Kayaking the Keys

Florida A&M University, Tallahassee
Florida Atlantic University, Boca Raton
Florida Gulf Coast University, Ft. Myers
Florida International University, Miami
Florida State University, Tallahassee
University of Central Florida, Orlando
University of Florida, Gainesville
University of North Florida, Jacksonville
University of South Florida, Tampa
University of West Florida, Pensacola

Kayaking the Keys

50 Great Paddling Adventures
in Florida's Southernmost Archipelago

Kathleen Patton

University Press of Florida

Gainesville · Tallahassee · Tampa · Boca Raton

Pensacola · Orlando · Miami · Jacksonville · Ft. Myers

07 06 05 04 03 02   6 5 4 3 2 1

All photographs were taken by the author, unless otherwise noted.

Library of Congress Cataloging-in-Publication Data
Patton, Kathleen.
Kayaking the Keys: 50 great paddling adventures in Florida's
southernmost archipelago / Kathleen Patton.
p. cm.
Includes index.
ISBN 0-8130-2579-6 (pbk.: alk. paper)
1. Sea kayaking—Florida—Florida Keys—Guidebooks. 2. Florida Keys
(Fla.)—Guidebooks. I. Title.
GV776.F62 F568 2002
797.1'224—dc21   2002027132

The University Press of Florida is the scholarly publishing agency
for the State University System of Florida, comprising Florida A&M
University, Florida Atlantic University, Florida Gulf Coast University,
Florida International University, Florida State University, University
of Central Florida, University of Florida, University of North Florida,
University of South Florida, and University of West Florida.

University Press of Florida
15 Northwest 15th Street
Gainesville, FL 32611-2079
http://www.upf.com

Contents

Illustrations

Figures

Maps

Tables

Preface

This book is a guide to exploring the Florida Keys by kayak. It includes a few short trips suitable for beginners and children, many half-day trips, and a few all-day excursions and overnight trips. Fifty trips are suggested, covering an array of natural environments. They span the entire island chain, from north of Key Largo to west of Key West.

Kayaking here is low-key. Hazards common in northern waters—strong tidal surges, water so cold it can kill you within minutes, freighter traffic, fog, huge floating deadhead logs—are not a part of the local picture. Our seas are shallow and gin clear, and there is often more to see under the waves than above them. The water is not dark and mysterious; it's absolutely beautiful and utterly transparent. So kayaking in the Keys is fundamentally different than it is in most other parts of the United States.

We prefer open, sit-upon kayaks, ones in which seawater flows in and out around the paddler. They are slower and less sleek, shorter and technically simpler than classic cockpit-style kayaks. We use them because one of the main reasons for kayaking these tropical waters is not to stay in a boat on the water but to leave it. Our kayaks take us to snorkeling spots, patch reefs, swimming holes, and pristine sandbars. Some local paddlers wouldn't think of launching without scuba gear aboard. You can race if you want, or paddle all day, or string together several of the trips in this book to cover more territory, but most kayakers here relax and pause often. They look down a lot because there is so much to see beneath their hulls—manatees, dolphins, brilliant tropical reef fish, coral heads, sponges, sea stars, sharks, and rays.

You will see kayaks atop many cars here and in many backyards. For those paddlers who already have favorite routes and destinations, this book offers new choices. For visitors to the Keys it gives an introduction to our region and a sampling of places to explore by sit-upon or cockpit kayak or, in many cases, by canoe. And for those who have never been in a kayak but who enjoy swimming, snorkeling, diving, birding, outdoor exercise, regional history, or new travel venues, it offers a unique way of touring an area of startling beauty and diversity.

Our low-lying mangrove islands are deceptive—unremarkable from a distance, yet teeming with life upon closer inspection. They also form a bewildering maze, one that this book hopes to celebrate and partially decipher. Maps are offered alongside the text. Used in conjunction with nautical charts, compass work, and careful observation, they should help any paddler feel less adrift.

Kayaking, although immensely rewarding, is not without risks. This book is intended as a guide, not a guarantee. To maximize your enjoyment and safety on the water, familiarize yourself with safe boating practices and proceed cautiously.

When you live on an island, you can't help but take to the sea. Thanks to all who have paddled these waters with me—Jim, Geri, Ross, Kate, Will, and Mary, among others. Thanks also to Jim Bell of the National Key Deer Refuge and Jeff Klinkenberg of the *St. Petersburg Times* for their careful reading and comments. The easy-on-the-eye maps come courtesy of Jim Patton at Cane Bayou—top of the charts.

1

Why Kayaking the Keys?

Dangling off the southern coast of Florida, like a comma marking a pause in the long run-on sentence of twenty-first-century America, is a tropical archipelago stretching 150 miles. Its thousand-hued shallow waters are a respite from the world of cell phones and superhighways. They also offer some of the best paddling opportunities in the United States. Nearshore waters and tidal creeks provide children and novices with safe and rewarding day trips, while open ocean routes and trips to coral patch reefs reward seasoned paddlers looking for excitement and adventure.

The kayak seems uniquely tailored to the clear, shallow waters of the Florida Keys, and it offers a vantage point that is far superior to that offered by colossal cruise ships and high-speed powerboats and Jet Skis. For if you can have a 360-degree view of the world from aboard these vessels on a clear day, then you'll need a new geometry to calculate the view you can have over these transparent waters from a kayak—360 degrees above and around you, and another 360 degrees below. You will not likely see your reflection. You will see something new, something that never was as it is right now, something that will never be that way again. Something bold, or subtle, or remarkable. In my years kayaking these waters I've seen things I never imagined:

Last spring a teenager and I were paddling through aquamarine waters less than a mile from Marathon, Florida. We were happy and warm and fully engaged in our conversation. Then, like the burst of a rocket, a spotted eagle ray leapt clear out of the water, unfurling his six-foot black polka-dotted "wings" and flaunting ivory belly before flying back into the water less than five feet from our kayaks. We stared, mouths agape, riveted to the moment.

On another occasion I paddled through a series of mangrove tunnels to the interior of a crescent-shaped islet. There was no wind at all, and the sun shone intensely. I pulled and drifted my way through the tangled mangroves, admiring brightly colored spiral tree snails. I kept a wary eye on the pincers of tree crabs just above my ears as the water got shallower and shallower, until there was just an inch or so under my hull. The tunnels gave out onto a small lagoon. Black mangroves grew tall on the banks. They were festooned with squawking ibises and herons who looked too heavy for the pliant branches. I pulled up my paddle and looked into the water. All around me it pulsed with life as hundreds, perhaps thousands, of celadon green upside-down jellyfish fluttered their tentacles in, then out, in a continuous movement that was totally silent and primordial.

Near West Washerwoman patch reef late one summer afternoon a friend and I came across large masses of sargassum. We had to dig to get through each clump and speed up our paddling when we sighted a mass on the horizon so that we could float at least part of the way across it. When we bogged down, we used our paddles as specimen trays, scooping up hunks of the dense seaweed. Then carefully, slowly, we separated its threads, revealing tiny brittle sea stars, tube worms, and here and there a baby ballyhoo (fish). I remembered another friend telling me that she knew someone who had once found a tiny sailfish in such a clump. A baby sailfish that she held in her hands. Imagine that.

Kayaking the Keys makes for an unforgettable vacation in the only tropical islands that can be reached by car from the American mainland. And, for those of us who live here, kayaking provides an affordable, enjoyable way to explore the waters that surround our island homes. The beauty of kayaking the Keys for locals and visitors alike lies not only in seeing exotic scenery but in developing a unique way of looking at the world around us.

From a kayak everything seems at once both grand and minuscule— the immensity of the sea and the infinite smallness of a grain of desiccated cactus algae lying at the bottom of a tidal slough.

One glimpse of a shark reminds you of your place in the food chain. A double rainbow arching across the whole sky from Florida Bay to the Atlantic Ocean puts even that in perspective.

1. Conch shell, symbol of the Florida Keys

What You Can Expect

The Keys are a gentle place. Except during tropical storms and hurricanes, it's possible to kayak year-round here. When cold fronts push down in the winter months, winds may reach twenty-five miles an hour, but they usually die down within a day or two. You can often fit in a short paddle even on these blustery days if you keep in the lee of the wind or seek out protected mangrove tunnels near shore. Spring and early summer bring ideal paddling weather with long daylight hours, temperatures in the seventies and eighties, and gentle seas. Summer's heat may keep you off the water during the day, but early morning and sunset trips offer not only tranquil beauty but a chance to dive patch reefs without the hassle of wet suits and scuba tanks. What is called autumn in other parts of the United States is my favorite time of all. As the angle of the sun's rays grows longer on the horizon, a golden glow plays on the water. Migrating birds return to their roosts in the mangroves. Watching the luminescent

Protected Areas

Today much of the land and water in the Florida Keys is protected by state and federal mandate and by acquisition by environmental organizations such as the Nature Conservancy. While paddlers will appreciate restrictions on Jet Skis in many of these areas, we must also do our part to protect these fragile habitats:

- Familiarize yourself with marine sanctuary and refuge regulations and boundaries.
- Stay off beaches in the backcountry areas of the Great White Heron, National Key Deer, and Key West National Wildlife Refuges.
- Don't camp on backcountry islands except at designated campsites in Everglades National Park.
- Don't collect or disturb coral, sea whips, or sea fans.
- Keep well away from nesting birds and sea turtles.
- Learn and obey the new guidelines for snorkeling in waters surrounding Dry Tortugas National Park.

orb of a harvest moon rise over the ocean as you rock on the waves is magical.

The moon's phase affects tidal range, of course, but the pull of the tides is less pronounced in the Keys than in other popular kayaking areas, such as the Pacific Northwest or Canada. Tides vary by two feet or less on average here, making it easier to plan trips and prolong your time on the water.

Getting in and out of the water is easy in the Keys, too. There are plenty of public and private boat launches near good kayaking waters. Many offer kayak rentals as well (see individual trip descriptions). Because the Keys are a chain of islands linked by U.S. Highway 1, potential kayak launch sites are virtually anywhere there's enough room to pull off onto the shoulder of the road (without trespassing on private property). Like most kayakers here, I drive with one eye on the road and the other on the water. Where there's access, there's adventure.

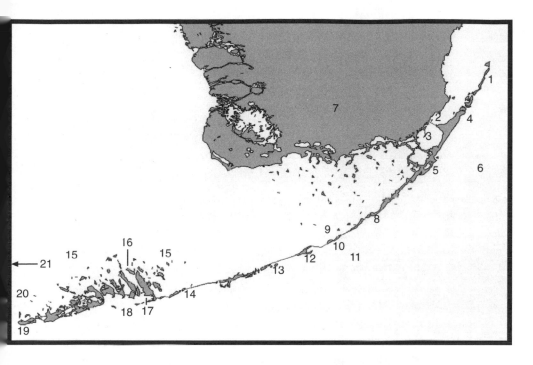

1.1. Public Lands in the Florida Keys: (1) Biscayne National Park; (2) Biscayne Bay/Card Sound Aquatic Preserve; (3) Crocodile Lake National Wildlife Refuge; (4) Dagny Johnson Key Largo Hammocks Botanical State Park; (5) John Pennekamp Coral Reef State Park; (6) Key Largo National Marine Sanctuary; (7) Everglades National Park; (8) Windley Key Fossil Reef Geological State Park; (9) Lignumvitae Key Botanical State Park; (10) Indian Key Historic State Park; (11) San Pedro Underwater Archaeological Preserve State Park; (12) Long Key State Park; (13) Curry Hammock State Park; (14) Bahia Honda State Park; (15) Great White Heron National Wildlife Refuge; (16) National Key Deer Refuge; (17) Coupon Bight Aquatic Preserve; (18) Looe Key National Marine Sanctuary; (19) Fort Zachary Taylor Historic State Park; (20) Key West National Wildlife Refuge; (21) Dry Tortugas National Park (not shown on map; 70 miles west of Key West)

Marinas and boat launches are busier, of course, especially on weekends. Compared with other boating areas, however, they are wonderfully uncrowded. And most powerboats and sailboats aren't going where kayakers go, anyway. They head "out front" to fish and dive the reef or off to the backcountry via the channels that skirt the shoals. You'll see flats fishermen poling their boats or perhaps a sponger working the hardbottom areas. If you feel too crowded, seek shallower water or pull your boat up on a sandbank and enjoy your own private beach. It will disappear when the tide rises and, if you've timed your trip right, you'll have an easy paddle back to shore.

The Florida Keys provide many trips for those paddlers who want a break from the stress of modern life or for naturalists who want to silently observe birds or marine life up close. Short trips near shore are also a great chance for novice kayakers to get comfortable with their gear, learn how to navigate using a marine chart and compass, or try something new—like fishing from a kayak.

More advanced kayakers can venture farther from shore, enjoying the diversity of Keys habitat. The backcountry offers intimate mangrove tunnels, open flats, and intricate mazes of tidal streams winding through tiny islets. "Out front" in the Atlantic there are patch reefs to explore and waves to ride. It's even possible to transport a kayak aboard a ferry to the Dry Tortugas, seventy miles west of Key West, to explore several keys at the far reach of this archipelago. Here the long-armed octopus and other behemoths make their home. It's a wild, unforgettable place to visit.

A Look Around

The Keys are a chain of low-lying islands that run in a southwestward arc 135 miles long, from south of Miami to the Dry Tortugas seventy miles west of Key West. They are usually referred to as the Upper, Middle, and Lower Keys. Each section includes several distinct but mutually interdependent environments. As you kayak through the warm, translucent waters that surround these tropical isles, take time to enjoy the view.

The Ground beneath You

You are standing on a coral reef. Yes, even when you're in your street clothes, feet solidly planted on terra firma, the soil beneath your feet is a thin layer of sediment deposited on a fossilized reef laid down 120,000 years ago. As the vast glaciers that marked the Ice Age advanced from the north, sea levels in south Florida fell, and what had once been a reef became dry land, which in time was covered with a thin layer of organic matter. The fringing reef that lies five to seven miles offshore of today's Keys became separated from this dry land when the seas once again rose 7,000 years ago.

If you're in the Upper or Middle Keys (Key Largo to Bahia Honda) or Big Pine Key, the bedrock beneath you is Key Largo limestone. If you're in the Lower Keys (from Middle Torch to Key West), the rock under your feet is Miami oolite. Differences in the porosity of these two types of limestone greatly affect the plant and animal communities found on individual keys through the island chain. Two other key factors are elevation and the availability of fresh water. The highest point in the Florida Keys is just eighteen feet above sea level—a sobering thought when hurricane storm surges have run in excess of eighteen feet. Most Keys average less than ten feet in elevation.

Hardwood hammocks grow on the highest land. These tropical forests contain trees and plants common in the West Indies—mahogany, gumbo-limbo, lignum vitae, and two highly toxic ones, poisonwood and manchineel, considered to be one of the most poisonous trees in the world. They also contain much beauty, from brilliantly colored endangered tree snails to rare ferns, air plants such as bromeliads, native butterfly and vanilla orchids, night-blooming tree cacti, a large and varied population of butterflies, migrating South American songbirds, and the whitecrowned pigeon, which is found nowhere else in the United States. Tropical hardwood hammocks occur predominantly in the Upper and Middle Keys where the bedrock of Key Largo limestone is porous and water leeching through it produces many pits or solution holes. Outstanding examples of this rare ecosystem include Dagny Johnson Key Largo Hammocks Botanical State Park, off Cardsound Road on Key Largo, and Lignumvitae Key Botanical State Park, south of Islamorada.

Pine rockland forest occurs only in the Lower Keys and in a few isolated areas of the Everglades. The best example of this habitat can be found on Big Pine and parts of adjacent No Name Key. It is more open than hardwood hammocks and more heavily dominated by one species—slash pine trees. Saw palmetto, tropical shrubs and flowers, and grasses common on the Florida peninsula also grow here, part of a unique pine rockland ecosystem that is globally endangered. Today much of these two islands is owned and regulated by the federal government as part of the National Key Deer Refuge.

Freshwater wetlands, extremely rare in the Florida Keys, also occur on Big Pine and No Name Key, as well as on neighboring Big and Middle Torch, Cudjoe, Sugarloaf, and Little Knockemdown Keys. Buttonwood trees, saw palmettos, cattails, and leather fern all grow here. This is the heart of today's Key deer habitat, which once stretched from the Seven Mile Bridge all the way to Key West.

Mangroves thrive throughout the Keys because they can survive in salt water. These trees are so prolific here and so vital to the environment that they might even be considered an emblem of the Keys. Mangrove thickets extend from mudflats near shore to the edges of pine rockland forests and tropical hardwood hammocks. Mangroves are land builders, using their roots to trap sediment borne across Florida Bay from the mainland. In so doing they have formed more than two hundred islands in the Bay, many of which are "overwash islands" so low that they are routinely flooded by salt water. These provide a perfect roosting, feeding, and nesting environment for wading birds such as herons, egrets, ibis, roseate spoonbills, and pelicans, as well as for magnificent frigate birds, ospreys, and bald eagles. Yellow warblers, black-whiskered vireos, and mangrove cuckoos also flit among the dense vegetation.

Mangroves are able to survive in salt water because they have evolved mechanisms for screening out salt as they take up water through their roots and for excreting salt through their leaves. Red mangroves, which line virtually every shore in the Keys, rest on large arched prop roots that also help the tree to breathe in the oxygen-poor submerged "soil" near shore. These prop roots, a common sight for kayakers, protect the shoreline from storms and filter out heavy metals and undesirable nutrients from the runoff generated by the Keys' growing human population.

2. Red mangrove with prop roots

While they filter out many harmful substances, the prop roots also trap nutrients that are vital food for an amazing array of species. These include marine algae, baitfish, shrimp, juvenile fish of many species, mangrove snappers, crabs, and West Indian spiny lobsters, which live among mangrove roots until they're two years old. Filtering nearshore waters not only provides food for these species but also allows sunlight to penetrate the water, aiding marine plants that rely on photosynthesis.

Black mangroves root farther inland. Instead of prop roots they have many pencil-shaped pneumatophores (breathing roots) that poke out of submerged soil near the high-tide line. These too filter nearshore water. They thrive in saltwater marshes and scrub forests, forming nearly impenetrable masses. The undersides of their leaves are often white with encrusted salt, which they have pushed up and out—a unique means of adapting to a saline environment. White mangroves occur even farther inland. Although salt-tolerant, they appear more treelike, with thick, rounded leaves and no visible breathing roots. Researchers have documented that 60 percent of shallow-water mangroves were destroyed between 1955 and 1985. Today, with a growing appreciation of their role in land building, water filtration, and sustaining marine, animal, and bird life, mangroves are protected. Mangroves can be seen lining the bayside shores of nearly every island in the Florida Keys.

Mangrove tunnels are narrow tidal streams and dredged canals covered entirely by a canopy of mangroves. They are a joy to paddle—quiet, intimate, teeming with birds and fish. Good examples of this habitat include the tunnels off Dusenbury Creek near Barnes Sound north of Key Largo, where manatees can sometimes be spotted, and Perky Creek off Sugarloaf Key.

Natural beaches are rare in the Florida Keys, especially in the Upper Keys. They tend to occur on the southern and eastern shores of the Middle and Lower Keys, but are most prevalent in the Marquesas and the Dry Tortugas and on Boca Grande and Woman Key west of Key West. Unlike the quartz beaches that exist in the continental United States, Keys beaches are composed of coral broken off from offshore and patch reefs, coralline algae, and shell fragments. They glisten white (not beige) under the tropical sun, against a background of turquoise water. Coconut and silver thatch palms sway overhead while sea grapes and sea oats hold the shifting sands in place. Fiddler crabs and burrowing owls take refuge from the day's heat by digging in the sand. On summer nights marine turtles, especially hawksbills and loggerheads, lay their clutches of eggs above the high-tide line. Keys beaches are fragile places, subject to overdevelopment by builders, obliteration by storm surges, and pollution from careless beachgoers and offshore boaters, including cruise ships. Their beauty is undeniable and their attraction for kayakers immense. Among the loveliest beaches in the Keys are those at Curry Hammock State Park, Sombrero Beach in Marathon, Bahia Honda State Park, Boca Chica Key, and Dry Tortugas National Park.

Rocky shores seem almost anticlimactic in comparison to beaches, yet they too are an integral part of the Keys ecosystem. Here the exposed limestone bedrock has been eroded by waves and chemical action, leaving jagged shores full of crevices. Sea urchins, chitons, and other small marine organisms thrive in these crevices, providing an important food source for shorebirds. Plantation Key and the Money Keys—visible from the Seven Mile Bridge—have rocky shorelines. Kayakers must be very careful on and near the extremely sharp rocks that constitute this environment. They can easily damage plastic kayaks.

The Water around You

From the vantage point of a kayak, the Keys' shorelines, beaches, and forests are background scenery. Another world is closer at hand, a watery realm with its own distinct, interrelated habitats. All of the trips presented in this book feature paddling through relatively shallow water. The Florida Keys sit atop the southern edge of what geologists call the Florida Platform. This is a flat limestone base covered by less than three hundred feet of salt or brackish water, separating the Atlantic Ocean from the Gulf of Mexico.

The area north and northwest of the Keys, part of Florida Bay, is known locally as the backcountry. Its waters average less than twenty feet deep and consist of a seamless series of shallow saltwater lakes separated at low tide by hundreds of mudflats and shoals. More than two hundred mangrove islands are scattered throughout the backcountry. The sea bottom here includes three distinct marine habitats—seagrass meadows, hardbottom communities, and (rare) patch reefs. This jewel-like region is a premier kayaking destination.

On the other side of the Keys archipelago lies the Atlantic Ocean, known locally as "out front." The continental shelf here descends very gradually for more than five miles. Like the backcountry, the ocean's bed includes seagrass meadows, hardbottom communities, and (many) patch reefs. A much larger, two-hundred-mile-long fringing coral reef runs parallel to the Keys some seven miles from shore. While this outer reef is too far to reach safely in a kayak, it is a vital part of the Keys' ecosystem, and virtually all organisms that inhabit it can be seen on the trips described in this book. On the far southern side of the outer reef lie the Florida Straits, which push 6.5 million cubic yards of warm Caribbean water per second up through the Gulf Stream.

Whether in the backcountry or "out front," as a kayaker you will glide over exceptionally clear, warm waters. As you do so, let the water's surface act as a magnifying glass—or don a mask and flippers—and peer into three unusual communities flourishing just below your boat.

Seagrass meadows, more than two thousand square miles of them, grow on the bottom of Florida Bay and the neighboring Gulf of Mexico. The most common species in this habitat is turtle grass, a flat ribbonlike grass whose rhizomes extend five feet into the sea floor, anchoring the plant firmly in the soft submarine mud. Rounder-tipped manatee grass and pointy-leafed shoal grass also grow in these meadows. Each helps to thwart tidal erosion and decrease turbidity in shallow waters. Seagrasses are true grasses that have adapted to a saltwater environment. They provide nourishment and shelter for a wide variety of marine life including, as their names suggest, marine turtles and manatees. Reef fish frequent seagrass beds at night to feed, then retreat to the shelter of the reef's ledges and crevices. Many species of fish important to both commercial and recreational fishermen use the seagrass meadows as nurseries. They are a major feeding ground for lobsters, pink shrimp, snappers, red drum, and conchs. Southern stingrays and spotted eagle rays cruise through these waters. Wading birds are a common sight in this area too, standing stiltlike in the soft mud, ready to jab their beaks into the seagrass in search of small fish or other prey.

Because seagrass meadows occur in shallow, nearshore waters, as a kayaker you will spend much of your time in this habitat. Attune your eyes to the lightning-fast movement of stingrays, which will flash from their resting places on the sea bottom as the shadow of your boat appears. Scan the horizon for what look like floating logs; they are more apt to be sea turtles surfacing to breathe. Look, too, among the blades of grass for furry brown sea cucumbers, swimming blue crabs, and small mollusks. Needlefish are common here, resembling transparent pencils with green fins. Sometimes the sun's angle and their coloration make houndfish

Sharks!

See that dorsal fin poking through the water off your starboard side? If it's summer it could well be a tarpon, a glistening five-foot game fish weighing more than a hundred pounds, hence nicknamed the "silver king." More likely it's a shark. The most common sharks sighted in nearshore waters are bonnetheads, usually less than three feet long, with a distinctive round, almost semicircular head. Nurse sharks are plentiful, too. It's quite common to paddle right over these relatively large sharks, even in very shallow water, without either you or the shark noticing it. They are quiet, docile fish who prefer resting on the seafloor. Lemon sharks are among the most beautiful big fish, light gray-brown with a yellowish cast.

There are more than three hundred species of sharks in the world, only twenty-seven of which are considered dangerous. Nationwide, fifty to seventy shark attacks are reported each year, and fatalities from sharks are rare. Still, mythology and movies have combined to make our pulses race at the mere sight of a shark.

Simple precautions can prevent sharks from mistaking you for their real prey, fish:

- Don't swim in murky water or at sunrise or sunset.
- Don't spearfish—and if you do, never carry the fish you spear in a bag underwater.
- Don't wear shiny jewelry when swimming, snorkeling, or diving. Sharks can mistake this for fish.
- Never feed sharks, as some unscrupulous dive operators have begun to do.

One hundred sixty million sharks are killed by humans each year for food, aphrodisiacs, and sport. It is they, not we, who swim at the greater risk.

hard to spot, but if you're lucky you will see them rise up and dance through the water on their tails. If you see the water erupt into a rain of what looks like silver droplets falling upward, you have just witnessed a school of silversides—tiny fish fleeing a predator.

Hardbottom communities look like deserts under the sea, especially in comparison to luxuriant seagrass meadows and coral reefs. Through the lens of clear nearshore waters they are a dramatic and exotic sight. Hardbottom communities exist in marine areas where less than one inch of sediment covers the limestone seafloor. They are quite common in the backcountry and occur in oceanside waters less than sixteen feet deep. Often they owe their existence to strong tidal currents which routinely sweep all sediment from the seafloor, but they also occur naturally in less turbulent areas within half a mile of shore.

Sponges, soft corals, and sea fans thrive in this environment, much to the delight of kayakers. Loggerhead sponges are among the most spectacular, resembling beige truck tires up to three feet in diameter. A careful look inside will often disclose tiny colorful reef fish, shrimp, and even lobsters taking shelter there. Vase sponges are another beautiful sight, their triangular shapes sitting like pottery on a limestone shelf. Black bleeding sponges, cake sponges, and tube sponges also lie scattered on the hardbottom floor. Fire sponges are lovely but painful. Their bright orange flesh, often growing on the submerged prop roots of red mangroves, contains spikes that can burn your skin for hours.

Stony corals are another natural wonder found in this underwater desert. Their names indicate their shapes—golfball, finger, knobby brain coral. Soft corals such as sea fans, sea whips, and sea plumes in shades of purple and yellow provide a distinctly tropical look. Reef fish often dart among these corals, even in nearshore waters. They are particularly plentiful in solution holes, depressions that formed when the limestone bedrock was exposed to rainwater during the Ice Age. Angelfish, parrotfish, blue tangs, yellowtails, and doctorfish often take shelter here.

Invertebrates such as shrimp, lobsters, conch, and crabs also thrive in hardbottom communities. Live sand dollars and sea biscuits, with their furry brown spines, look far different from their smooth ivory skeletons that wash ashore on beaches. Live pencil urchins, too, look very different covered with long spines than they do as fragile purple seashells. Starfish, on the other hand, lose only their coloration when they die. Still, the sight of a Bahama cushion starfish, brilliantly red and nearly a foot in diameter, is a delight for kayakers. These beautiful starfish have been collected for hundreds of years and are now endangered. Federal and state fines are levied against those who collect them or the endangered queen conch.

Patch reefs are the only part of the Keys' famous reef system accessible to kayakers. The main coral reef in the Florida Keys is a fringing reef that parallels the Atlantic coast and lies between five and seven miles offshore. It is the only coral reef in the United States, largely because coral grows only in nutrient-poor, clear, sunlit water with a minimum temperature of sixty-eight degrees and depths less than two hundred feet. Reefs, dubbed "rainforests of the seas" by some scientists, are fragile ecosystems of great complexity created by millions of tiny organisms called polyps. Thousands of polyps are needed to build a single coral. They do so out of self-interest. Aided by single-celled algae that live within their tissues, the coral polyps, soft-bodied organisms related to jellyfish and sea anemones, extract calcium carbonate from seawater and use the mineral to build tube-shaped skeletons for their own protection. Few people ever see these mighty reef-builders, because they venture out of their skeletal casings only at night to feed on plankton. When they die, their skeletal remains are pressed together by the action of waves and the secretions of marine algae, building a solid structure that can extend from the seafloor to the water's surface. Coral grows at an excruciatingly slow pace, in most cases only inches a year. This helps to explain why it has taken more than forty species of coral—as well as organisms such as foraminifera, bryozoans, polychaete worms, and mollusks—6,500 years to build this two-hundred-mile-long reef.

More than 650 species of fish make the Keys' coral reefs their home. Most are brilliantly colored fish with striking geometric designs found only in the tropics. They include queen and French angelfish, rock beauties, spotfin butterfly fish, stoplight and queen parrotfish, and the ethereal midnight parrotfish. Blue tangs, queen triggerfish, tiny clownfish, and damselfish. Massive schools of porkfish and yellowtail snappers. Great barracuda and several species of sharks. Loggerhead, green, and Kemp's Ridley sea turtles. Moray eels hidden within coral crevices. Spotted eagle rays flying through the water, flapping their six-foot wings.

And what's more, all of these amazing creatures can be seen by kayakers who paddle just far enough offshore to explore a patch reef. These are small remnants of the outer reef, which once extended from the modern shore of the Keys to the present-day fringe reef. Several trips outlined in this book venture to these miniature reefs with maximum beauty.

The Sky above You

Kayakers may be the luckiest of all boaters. Because we travel slowly and propel ourselves with our own steady motions, we can look around us—and below and above us—as we glide through the water. We won't run aground or foul our lines if we decide on a whim to throw our heads back and stare at the sky, not just for a moment but for as long as we feel like it.

The skies above the Florida Keys are unimaginably interesting and beautiful. In winter they tend to be clear and blue, sometimes marked by high cirrus clouds but little else.

Birds of a stunning diversity, hundreds of species, overwinter or make their permanent homes here. As a kayaker, especially amid the mangrove islands of the backcountry, you are bound to see flocks and rookeries of water birds such as brown pelicans, cormorants, white and glossy ibis, and members of the heron family—the great blue heron and great white heron (a color morph of the blue), great egret, snowy egret, little blue heron, green heron, and beautiful yellow-crowned night heron. If you are fortunate and seek out the right islands between November and April, you may catch the amazing sight of a roseate spoonbill—flamingo pink wings and orange tail set against a deep blue sky, its long round bill and three-foot frame stretched out in flight.

Ospreys are a more common but still delightful sight. These fish hawks fly high over the backcountry and are easy to identify because of their dark brown body and white breast. The short-tailed hawk, known locally as the klee-klee, is another common raptor. Bald eagles can be seen soaring and gliding along high air currents or perched atop old trees, their black bodies, white heads, and large size an aid in identification. Curry Hammock State Park reportedly has one of the world's highest concentrations of peregrine falcons during their fall migration, and I have seen one nestled on a ledge at Fort Jefferson in the Dry Tortugas, seventy miles from any other land mass.

Magnificent frigate birds can also be seen far from shore. These are agile, high-flying birds with a striking appearance. Both sexes are jet black, with long, deeply forked tails. Adult females can be identified by their white breasts, while males have black breasts and distinctive bright red balloon pouches under their bills, which they inflate only near their nests.

Shorebirds such as sandpipers, ruddy turnstones, and snipes patrol the beaches, and flocks of seagulls and sandwich terns are common near shore. Bird-watchers themselves flock to the Dry Tortugas, lifetime bird lists in hand, to view sooty tern and brown noddy colonies in their remote breeding grounds.

Mangrove cuckoos, white-crowned pigeons, and burrowing owls live in the Keys year-round. Other species, especially song birds, fly here to overwinter, and exotic South American and Caribbean species both migrate here and are blown in by strong weather systems.

Fat Albert, another sight common to Florida Keys kayakers, is also affected by strong weather. A huge Naval Air blimp tethered with a 1,400-foot line to his base on Cudjoe Key, Fat Albert can be seen high in the sky on any clear day from most backcountry waters. He is a strange sight, a mammoth white blimp on a ribbonlike leash. Fat Albert picks up a fat federal paycheck for a stealthy mission—drug surveillance using highly sophisticated electronics. Rumor has it that he can also read a license plate in Old Havana. His twin brother beams transmissions of TV Martí, a call to arms from the U.S. government to the people of Cuba, ninety miles away.

When foul weather looms, Fat Albert and his brother are brought down for shore leave. (Once, he was actually shot down by naval riflemen because he had broken free from his tether.) On clear days he provides a surreal sight reminiscent of *The Truman Show*, and a very visible point of reference for kayakers adrift amid the mangrove isles.

Rainbows offer aerial wonders of another sort on rainy days. Formed when sunlight is refracted and reflected by water droplets suspended in the air, these lovely and intriguing sky sights occur most often during the summer rainy season. Rainbows are most common early in the morning and late in the afternoon. Because a rainbow looks bigger when other features of the landscape, like trees and houses, are farther away, viewing them from a kayak offers spectacular results, especially in these low-lying mangrove islands. Multiple rainbows are a fairly common sight here, but the view of one or more rainbows arching over both sides of an island, from the backcountry to the ocean, is truly unforgettable.

The next time you see a rainbow (or two), consider this:

· If you see more than one rainbow, the colors of the first rainbow will run from red on the outside to violet on the inside, but those of the second, double rainbow will be in reverse order.

· When a rainbow spans both fresh and salt water, its appearance will shift because the rainbow angle for seawater is .8 degrees smaller than that for fresh water.

· People who have had cataract surgery and have aphakic eyes are able to see a broader ultraviolet component—and a better rainbow—than people with "normal" vision.

· And that pot of gold at the end of the rainbow? Treasure from a Spanish shipwreck is still rumored to be near Pelican Shoal, and divers in the Marquesas did find the *Atocha*'s gold and emeralds.

The Green Flash is a phenomenon you're bound to hear of if you spend more than a few days in the Keys. There is, after all, a cocktail named after it, and it seems to be a mainstay of conversation, particularly among mariners, from Key Largo to Key West. Perhaps this is because sunsets are a ritual event in the Keys. They are fabulous here, especially during the summer, and Key West has built an entire tourist economy around celebrating them. The green flash occurs most often as the sun sets, although it can occur at sunrise too. It is seen as a brief, brilliant green burst of light that usually lasts no more than a few seconds. It is a prismatic effect, the result of atmospheric refraction as the final top bit of the sun's orb descends below the horizon.

To see the green flash you must be lucky. It also helps if you are prepared. Choose a calm, clear evening, wear sunglasses, and position yourself so that you have an unrestricted view of the horizon—no buildings, trees, or clouds obstructing your view. You should have a clear line of sight for several miles all the way to the horizon. It is best if you can see the curvature of the Earth, as you can from a kayak or other boat on the water. (It is also best to have a viewpoint relatively high above the horizon. If you can safely stand in your kayak, do so just as the sun sets.) Hope for a sun that is yellow, not red, as it descends toward the horizon. As it sets, its circular form will seem to flatten more and more as it gets closer to the horizon. Notches will appear on either side of the sun. If you're lucky and conditions are perfect, these notches will come together just as the sun sinks below the waterline. As it sinks, its light is refracted, creating a continuum of images with different wavelengths and locations. Blue light has the shortest wavelength, and so the blue image of the sun occurs highest up on this continuum. Red, with its longer wavelength, occurs on the bottom. In a phenomenon called Rayleigh scattering (caused in large part by aerosol pollution), blue light scatters in the atmosphere. What's left is essentially a red setting sun with a sliver of green sun at its top. When the red sun sets, the green one flashes momentarily before disappearing into the sea. This is the famous green flash.

Don't fret if you miss this celestial event. For all the talk about it here in the Keys, it is actually best seen in polar regions where the sun skims along the horizon rather than truly setting. On his 1929 expedition to Little America, Admiral Byrd reported observing the green flash for thirty-five minutes.

L'Heure bleue is the French term to describe the hour after the sun sets, when a bluish cast descends on everything we see. If you're out in your kayak, particularly if you're on the ocean, you'll get a chance to experience this phenomenon to its fullest in the Florida Keys. As you dip your paddle and look into the water, then complete the stroke and look up, you'll see the line that normally separates sea from sky disappear. All you'll see is blue—some undulating with the surface of the waves, the rest becoming palpable, a satiny rendering of what only minutes ago seemed discrete and solid. This is a mystical time to be on the water.

2

Before Heading Out

What to Paddle

Plastic Sit-upon Kayaks

The boat best suited to the trips described in this guidebook is a plastic sit-upon kayak. Developed in the wake of the vastly popular plastic whitewater kayaks invented during the 1970s and the plastic sea kayaks that followed, this new breed of tropical kayak is perfect for the Keys. The boats are extremely lightweight—easy to strap onto a car rack or handcart, easy to launch, easy to portage over shoals or sharp coral rock, easy to scoot through "skinny water." Because the paddler sits in a molded seat scooped into the hull, he or she is free to leave at any time. There is no need to learn the Eskimo roll, and every reason to moor up to a buoy or mangrove bush and jump into the water for a free dive, or snorkel, or swim. Most important, a plastic sit-upon kayak keeps its paddler cool in this tropical climate. Water flows continuously through the seat section of the sit-upon, keeping the paddler cool on even the hottest days. And in this type of kayak, with some practice, you can even stand erect or use your paddle (or a pole) as a flats fisherman would for a better view (and cast) into nearshore waters.

Sit-upon kayaks are fairly similar in shape. In general, longer boats are faster and track better than smaller ones, but the latter are more maneuverable, especially in surf. Most kayaks are single, although two-person kayaks are popular with rental outfits. These tandem kayaks work well if you are paddling with a child or a person with physical or mental limitations, but single kayaks have clear advantages. They are much easier to maneuver in high wind and provide a greater sense of independence. Trying to paddle a tandem kayak by yourself is nearly impossible; seeing the landscape blocked by your partner's head can be frustrating.

Cockpit-Style Kayaks

Conventional cockpit-style sea kayaks can be paddled in the Keys, especially during the coldest months of December and January when the sea temperature is seventy degrees. Because the paddler sits below the waterline, these boats become quite uncomfortable from April through October, a prime kayaking season, when water temperatures exceed eighty degrees and air temperatures range from the eighties to the nineties. Cockpit kayaks are not recommended for diving or snorkeling trips.

Canoes

Canoes are suitable for many of the trips described in this book. However, while they are widely used in the Everglades and the waters off southwestern Florida, canoes are not safe for open ocean paddling. Once broached by a wave, they risk being sunk, and righting a canoe can be difficult. Furthermore, because canoes sit higher on the water, they present more surface area for strong winds to catch. Being swept out to sea is a distinct possibility during summer thunderstorms or frontal passages. Diving or snorkeling from a canoe is also not recommended (trust me, I've tried it). Canoes are, however, a good choice for paddling in tidal creeks or lagoons. Look for the canoe icon to designate the trips in this book that are appropriate.

Kayaks and canoes can be rented at several locations throughout the Keys. Rates and availability vary by vendor and season but average $20 an hour or $50 for the day. Look for the rental icon to designate the trips in this book that offer this service.

3. Sit-upon kayaks, perfect for the Keys

Kayak Care

Kayak owners should realize that the same sun that warms our water can, of course, break down the chemical composition of a plastic kayak, increasing its susceptibility to impact damage, especially from sharp coral and rocks. Without protection, this breakdown can happen in as little as three to six years. Applying a specially formulated sunscreen lotion to the kayak cuts down on such chemical degradation, as does storing your boat in the shade. Storing a boat on its gunwales rather than its hull also helps. Because warm weather can cause plastic kayaks to sag, it is also important to resist the temptation, however strong, to store your boat on your car's roof rack. The tropical sun here is intense, and plastic, ever so imperceptibly, melts.

Minor damage to a kayak can usually be repaired at home by melting strips of identically formulated (and colored) plastic available from the boat's manufacturer. Filling and sanding produces a mend that's both watertight and aesthetically pleasing. Major hull breaches, of course, are usually irreparable. So it's best to treat your kayak kindly.

Paddles

Paddles come in a variety of styles and sizes. Some are one piece, others pull apart for easy storage and can be used like canoe paddles in narrow tidal creeks or mangrove tunnels. The paddle shafts can be made of wood, fiberglass, or graphite. In general, the lighter the material, the easier it is to lift and push the paddle, but the more difficult it is to control in high wind or seas. The blades of paddles also vary in size and shape, with most being feathered—that is, having the blades set at an angle of sixty to ninety degrees from each other. Some kayakers prefer flat blades, while others prefer ones that are more spoon-shaped. In theory, the larger the blade, the more water displaced per stroke and hence the more power a kayaker has. Most paddles range in length from 220 to 230 centimeters. The kayaker's height and arm length and the width of the boat are the main determinants of what size paddle fits. The best way to ensure proper fit is to try several styles and lengths before heading out. Having the right paddle can make a huge difference in your comfort and speed. Even if you plan on renting a kayak, consider buying and traveling with your own paddle.

What to Pack

Necessities

Never leave shore without fresh water:

- Bring at least a quart of water per person for every four hours of your trip
- Drink some water every half hour, even if you're not thirsty

Sun protection is a must in the Keys:

- Wear a hat; a baseball-style cap of quick-dry nylon works well
- Wear polarized sunglasses, even on overcast days

- Wear waterproof sunscreen with both UVA and UVB protection; re-apply often, and don't forget to coat your feet if you're barefoot!

Clothing should be light and loose:

- Wear a swimsuit or quick-dry trunks
- Wear a loose, light-colored long-sleeved shirt
- Bring a towel, stored in a waterproof bag; it can cover your legs from sun, spray, and wind
- Wear water shoes to protect your feet from sharp objects and to make launching and portaging easier

Safety is your responsibility:

- Wear a life jacket (as required by the U.S. Coast Guard)
- File a float plan with a friend or at your lodging
- Bring a bilge pump
- Bring a whistle
- Bring a flashlight stored in a watertight bag, even on day trips
- Bring a marine radio on trips more than one mile offshore; a water-proof AM/FM, tuned to a local station for weather bulletins, is OK for shorter trips
- Bring flares on trips more than one mile offshore
- Bring six feet of sturdy rope, tied to the bow of your kayak and secured in several places along its deck
- Bring a simple waterproof first aid kit with bandages, aspirin, and meat tenderizer for jellyfish stings
- Bring insect repellent
- If you plan on snorkeling or diving, bring a dive flag that meets the new size regulations, and rigid framing to hoist it from your boat

Know the time and place:

- Bring a nautical chart of the area you're paddling in (see "How to Navigate" later in this chapter)

- Bring a compass
- Wear a waterproof watch, preferably one suited for diving
- Keep your car keys in a waterproof dive bag that floats, or wear them in a Velcro-sealed wrist wallet—after all, the purpose of your trip was to paddle, not to walk

Practice minimum-impact boating:

- Bring an active appreciation for the environment and a sense of awe and wonder
- Respect private and public property
- Take nothing but photos, leave nothing but bubbles

Amenities

The following items can make your trip more enjoyable:

- Watertight plastic dry bags
- Anchor (in case that mooring buoy you planned on tying up to is already taken)
- Extra paddle
- Collapsible kayak cart

Consider these lightweight means of recording your excursions:

- Disposable underwater camera
- Small notebook or sketchbook and pencil, stored in a zipped bag on deck

Enhance your explorations with field guides to the birds, fish, and sea life of the area. Here are some of the best:

- *The Sibley Guide to Birds,* by Daniel Allen Sibley
- *National Audubon Society Field Guide to North American Birds: Eastern Region*
- *National Audubon Society Field Guide to Tropical Marine Fishes*

- *National Audubon Society Field Guide to North American Seashore Creatures*
- *Coral Reefs of Florida,* by Gilbert L. Voss
- *Snorkeling Guide to Marine Life: Florida, Caribbean, Bahamas,* by Paul Humann and Ned DeLoach
- *Diving and Snorkeling Guide to the Florida Keys,* by John Halas, Judy Halas, and Don Kincaid
- *Florida Sportsman 2002 Fishing Planner* (revised annually to provide tide charts)

How to Navigate

Several annotated maps are included in this book. Individual trip descriptions provide detailed information about launch sites and landmarks along each route. The safest way to kayak the Keys, however, is to closely study the appropriate NOAA marine chart before and during your trip. Be sure to scrutinize your surroundings. Always find something "special" about your launch site that you can remember later on your return trip. Pay close attention to the contour of the islands and the depth and color of the water. Be especially mindful when you're paddling through tidal creek mazes.

Charts

Nautical charts published by NOAA (National Oceanic and Atmospheric Administration) show water depths, shoals, channels, and island contours in great detail. This information is essential for trips more than a mile offshore, for trips in the backcountry, and for snorkeling trips.

NOAA charts themselves can be rather large, and they're not waterproof. They are sold at marinas and retail stores throughout the country. A list of vendors is available from

Office of Coast Survey
1315 East West Highway
Silver Spring, MD 20910

NOAA charts can also be ordered by phone at 1-800-638-8972. NOAA maintains a very informative website at www.noaa.gov.

Waterproof charts based on NOAA data are sold individually for the Upper, Middle, and Lower Keys and can be purchased for $20 each from

Pasadena Hot Spot

4016 Strawberry Road

Pasadena, TX 77504

or online from www.waterproofcharts.com or www.maptech.com.

Standard Mapping Services produces great laminated charts with aerial photos that clearly show shoals, banks, channels, creeks, and more. They can be ordered directly from the company at (504) 898-0025.

Compass

It can be tough telling one mangrove island from another here in the Keys, and damn near impossible from three miles out in the backcountry. You'll need a compass, either a cheap plastic one or a fancier mariner's compass attached to your deck. Consult a chart and plot your course before launching, then check your heading from time to time. Depending on the tides, you may be able to plot a much more efficient course by paddling over shoals rather than avoiding them.

GPS

Global Positioning System devices can help you plot a course, save coordinates, and provide a permanent record of your trip. If you're carrying one, be sure to store it in a waterproof, floatable bag.

How to Read Keys Water

Skinny Water

The Keys are not subject to the huge tidal variations found in other areas popular with kayakers. On average, the tidal variation ranges from .2 feet in Florida Bay to 2.4 feet in the Atlantic. Nonetheless, understanding the tides and knowing how to calculate daily tidal stages and ranges is of critical importance to Keys kayakers for a very simple reason—mean low tides (the average lowest level of water at low tide in a particular place) can be only a few inches. Locals call this "skinny water." Venturing out at the wrong time can leave you high and dry, especially in the backcountry. What may have been an effortless paddle through a chain of mangrove islands can easily become a major inconvenience if you're stranded in water too skinny to float even your shallow-draft kayak. The sea bottom can be a gray mucky mess that will suck up your water shoes and make every portaging step a struggle. It can add hours to your trip even if you're "out front" in the Atlantic, because many deepwater channels there are surrounded by shoals and skinny-water flats—and from your low sitting position in a kayak it can sometimes be hard to read the water's colors and see these flats.

Like most places along the East and West Coasts of the United States, Keys waters experience two high and two low tides every day. But unlike most of these coastlines, where daily semidiurnal tides bring two high tides of roughly the same size and two low tides of the same size, Keys tides are mixed. This means that a particular day's two high tides can vary greatly in their height, and so can the low tides.

The height of each tide also differs according to such factors as the phase of the moon, the presence of strong winds, barometric pressure, and even the temperature of the water. Higher high tides and lower low tides occur in the three days before and after each full moon. This "spring tide" phenomenon is reversed by the "neap tide" effect during the moon's first and last quarter phases, when high and low tide variations are minimized. Strong, persistent winds also affect tidal variations year-round. Strong winds from the east, for example, blow water out of the backcountry into the Gulf of Mexico. The result can be extremely low tides and lots of skinny water. In some cases a strong east wind can even hold back an incoming tide, causing it to arrive later than is predicted on tide charts and to have a smaller volume of water. Seasonal variations in sea temperature and atmospheric pressure also affect tide heights. When the seawater is at its warmest it expands, causing a sea-level rise of as much as eight inches. Sea levels are at their highest in October; between November and February they fall off substantially. Barometric pressure can cause six-inch changes in the tides.

Further complicating the picture is the fact that the sea level is higher in the Gulf of Mexico than in the Atlantic Ocean. Because of this, the current flowing through natural and man-made channels from one side of the Keys to the other flows almost constantly from the Gulf to the ocean side. Most of the trips in this book avoid such channels altogether.

However, kayakers paddling out of the backcountry to Indian Key, the wreck of the *San Pedro*, the Money Keys, or the Molasses Keys may find themselves paddling on an outgoing current from the backcountry into an incoming tide on the ocean.

Tidal Currents

Currents at the northern edges of the backcountry can also pose challenges for kayakers. Here the tide pours in and out of shallow basins with great speed and force. This tidal effect is most pronounced in narrow tidal

---

Making Tidal Calculations

The only safe way to tell how much water you'll have under your hull on any given day's paddle is to consult the daily tide chart and make the necessary tidal difference calculations for your particular launch site, route, and destination.

First consult the local tide chart, available daily in local papers, on radio and television, and in yearly published fishing guides.

Then calculate the tidal adjustment for your put-in site using the Tidal Corrections Chart provided here. Differences are given in hours and minutes that should be added to or subtracted from the published daily tide charts for Miami Harbor or Key West, as indicated.

Calculate the daily high and low tides before every launch, remembering to note any possible effects from the moon, wind, or season.

Finally, make a good long study of the navigational chart, paying special consideration to areas less than three feet in depth. Plan on either being somewhere else during low tide in these areas or finding a sandy-bottomed bank (not a mucky gray marl flat) to while away the hours until the water level rises. And, if you decide to linger on your temporary beach, make sure to secure your boat somehow before the tide comes in.

In tidal stream areas (noted in the trip descriptions) the water rushes in quite rapidly. Be prepared.

Table 1. Tidal Corrections for Florida Keys Launch Sites

Location	Differences		Mean Low Tide Level
	High	Low	(feet)
Elliott Key Harbor	+2.19	+3.04 (on Miami)	0.83
Adams Key	+1.24	+1.12 (on Miami)	0.90
Barnes Sound	+5.37	+6.24 (on Miami)	0.25
Largo Sound	+2.36	+3.07 (on Miami)	0.47
Indian Key	−0.58	−0.35 (on Key West)	1.09
Shell Key	+0.31	+1.57 (on Key West)	0.33
Lignumvitae Key	+0.09	+1.31 (on Key West)	0.37
Long Key (lake)	+0.33	+0.57 (on Key West)	0.53
Fat Deer Key	−1.11	−0.36 (on Key West)	0.83
Boot Key (bridge)	−1.03	−0.37 (on Key West)	0.96
Molasses Key	−0.56	−0.16 (on Key West)	0.67
Money Keys	+0.03	+1.17 (on Key West)	0.54
Bahia Honda	−0.45	−0.27 (on Key West)	0.74
No Name Key (east)	+1.35	+1.33 (on Key West)	0.55
Big Pine Key (northeast)	+3.19	+2.30 (on Key West)	0.80
Big Pine Key (north)	+4.24	+5.56 (on Key West)	0.85
Newfound Harbor[a]	−0.41	+0.05 (on Key West)	0.76
Munson Island (reef)	−0.40	−0.12 (on Key West)	0.84
Big Torch (Niles)	+3.15	+2.05 (on Key West)	0.56
Content Keys	+2.47	+3.05 (on Key West)	1.87
Summerland Key (bridge)	−0.10	+0.56 (on Key West)	0.59
Knockemdown Key (north)	+3.30	+4.54 (on Key West)	1.19
Cudjoe Key (north)	+3.32	+4.40 (on Key West)	1.43
Sawyer Key (south)	+2.37	+5.19 (on Key West)	1.17
Perky Creek	+5.37	+8.25 (on Key West)	0.23
Snipe Point	+2.15	+3.33 (on Key West)	1.47

Location	Differences		Mean Low Tide Level
	High	Low	(feet)
Duck Key	+3.27	+4.57 (on Key West)	1.03
Shark Key (O'Hara)	+3.53	+5.39 (on Key West)	0.90
Saddlebunch Keys/Similar Sound	+0.39	+2.41 (on Key West)	0.31
Boca Chica Bridge	+1.23	+1.29 (on Key West)	0.52
Channel Key (west)	+3.09	+3.07 (on Key West)	0.62
Dry Tortugas (Garden Key)	+0.29	+0.33 (on Key West)	0.89

To use this chart:

Identify your launch site or destination in the first column.

Add or subtract the time (listed in hours and minutes—i.e., "5.37" means "5 hours, 37 minutes") to the high tides published for the day of your trip, using Miami Harbor or Key West as indicated. For example, if the high tides expected for a certain day at Miami Harbor are noon and 6 P.M., then the high tides for that date at Barnes Sound would be at 5:37 P.M. and 11:37 P.M.

Make similar calculations for the low tides published for the day of your trip.

Note that the lowest water level at low tide is indicated in the last column. (At Barnes Sound this low mean tide is only ¼ foot. Now that's skinny water!)

Remember that tidal current can be just as important as tidal height. Maximum tidal current occurs midway through an incoming or outgoing tide. Currents diminish closer to full high tide or low slack tide.

These statistics are taken from *Embassy Guides: Diving, Fishing, Boating in the Florida Keys*. More extensive tidal statistics are available from Reed's Nautical Companion website at www.reeds.com.

[a]Tides are as published for Ramrod Key on Newfound Harbor Channel. No figures are available for Little Torch on Newfound Harbor Channel. "Munson Island (reef)" refers to the patch reef in trip # 19.

creeks on the edge of the Gulf. Kayakers should avoid these areas when the tidal flow is greatest; otherwise they risk being swept into the Gulf. Generally speaking, a current reaches its maximum strength halfway through an incoming or outgoing tide. Therefore, kayakers should be most careful during this time.

How to Read Keys Weather

Tropical Weather Patterns

Key West lies only one degree of latitude above the Tropic of Cancer, the official northern boundary line of the tropics. All of the Florida Keys are "tropical" islands in that they have never experienced frosts or freezes. In general, they have a monsoonal climate characterized by a dry and a wet season. The rainy season extends from June through October. Most of the area's thirty-nine inches of rain falls during that time.

Each summer, moisture from the Gulf of Mexico, the Caribbean Sea, and the Atlantic Ocean fuels high humidity and the formation of clouds. Afternoon thunderstorms are common, bringing drenching rains and sometimes high winds. Lightning and waterspouts (miniature tornadoes that occur over open water) are the greatest dangers for kayakers venturing out during the summer months. It's imperative that you monitor weather forecasts in advance of launching and keep an eye on the sky for the formation of thunderheads. Shelter from storms is hard to come by in these low-lying mangrove islands and nonexistent over open water. The best defense against bad weather is forewarning. A NOAA (National Oceanographic and Atmospheric Agency) weather radio can be bought in most boating supply stores for less than $15. Current weather conditions for nearshore and offshore waters of the entire Keys region are updated hourly. For the Lower and Middle Keys, the frequency is 162.400 MHz or Band 2 on marine radios; for the Upper Keys, it is 162.450 MHz or Band 5.

Hurricanes

As a tropical region, the Florida Keys are also subject to the devastating impact of tropical storms and hurricanes. During the 112 years for which meteorological records have been kept, forty-seven hurricanes packing winds in excess of seventy-five miles an hour have passed within sixty-five miles of Marathon, midway down the island chain. Of these, twenty-four have been major hurricanes. The official hurricane season extends from June 1 to November 30. Historically, most hurricanes that have threatened the Keys have occurred from September through mid-October. Florida experiences two hurricanes a year on average.

A hurricane's power is hard to overestimate. The power generated by an average hurricane, if converted to electricity, could power the entire United States for six months. The Florida Keys, averaging less than ten feet above sea level, are particularly vulnerable to these storms' high winds, torrential rain, and tidal surge. The great Labor Day Hurricane of 1935 packed winds of two hundred miles per hour and an eighteen-foot tidal surge that swept the Overseas Railroad off its track and left eight hundred people dead. Even a much smaller storm, 1998's Hurricane Georges, caused millions of dollars in damage and destroyed one-quarter of the trees on Key West.

Meteorologists are able to predict the size, impact, and track of these storms much more accurately than in the past. Their predictions are widely reported by local media and marine radio and can thus inform your kayaking plans. But, if you are planning a trip to the Keys from another state or country, be sure to check south Florida weather conditions before you travel. (And, if you have secured your lodging accommodations by making a deposit, be sure to find out about cancellation and refund policies well in advance of your visit.) Campers should also note that national, state, and county parks are closed once tropical storm or hurricane watches are posted.

The Best Weather for Paddling

The end of hurricane season coincides with the start of the dry season. Average daytime temperatures are in the seventy-degree range and the dew point plunges. Rainfall averages less than two inches a month. This balmy weather is the source of the Keys' reputation as Paradise. Calm, clear days occur often throughout the winter months. Occasionally these glory days are interrupted by the passage of cold fronts from the mainland. During these events the trade winds which generally blow from the east and southeast are replaced by strong winds from the north and west.

Winds in excess of twenty-one knots blow about 10 percent of the time during this period. These winds rarely render kayaking an impossibility. They can, however, affect your choice of destinations.

If winds and waves are kicking up on the Atlantic, head for the back-country. If Turkey Basin is as hot as a kettle, go "out front." If northern winds race in from the mainland, stay in the ocean in the lee of the Keys. That's the beauty of living in the islands.

3

Kayak Trips in the Florida Keys

Paradise begins a quarter mile offshore.
—local Keys saying

Mile Markers

Access to the waters of the Florida Keys is off the two-lane highway that links forty-seven of the islands. The Overseas Highway, which is the southernmost section of U.S. 1, begins just south of Florida City, about twenty-five miles south of Miami. The entire route sports green metal mile-marker signs, beginning with MM 123 on the eighteen-mile stretch that links the mainland with Key Largo and ending at MM 1 on Truman Avenue in Key West. Virtually all directions given in the Keys start with "turn at MM number . . ." Although U.S. 1 descends in a southwesterly arc, it is customary to speak of going "up" or "down" the Keys. Directions also mention whether a destination is "bayside" (Gulf side) or "ocean-side."

The trips here are arranged in descending geographical order, starting with paddles in Biscayne National Park, reached by ferry from Homestead, just north of the MM grid. The next trip starts from MM 111. The last trips reachable by car are paddles in Key West, south of MM 1. The trips to Dry Tortugas National Park are reached by ferry, and are listed in nautical miles west of Key West.

Maps

Maps accompany the text, indicating each trip's route. Although based on NOAA charts, these maps show only the broad outlines of landmasses (in dark gray) and shoals (in light gray). No depth soundings or channel markers are shown.

Paddling Times

Paddling times stated for each trip are based on my own experience on solo and group trips in plastic sit-upon kayaks. The speed of these rudderless kayaks averages out to about two nautical miles an hour. Obviously, if you push yourself or paddle a cockpit-style kayak with a rudder, you'll go faster than this. If you're setting a more leisurely pace or are paddling with children, your time may be a bit slower. Finally, "paddling time" means just that—the time it takes to actually paddle to and from the trip's destination. It doesn't include time spent exploring areas not mentioned specifically in the text, or snorkel or swim time. In some cases you'll want to add an hour or more to fully enjoy your trip.

Trip Descriptions and Comments

This book is predominantly a how-to guide for kayaking in the Florida Keys. While it provides information on launch sites, distances, and notable features, it certainly doesn't claim to be a definitive guide, nor does it attempt to take away any paddler's sense of discovery. In fact, one of the most wonderful things about kayaking is that each trip is entirely fresh, entirely new because the sea changes constantly.

Notes

"Notes" differ from comments and trip descriptions in that they convey crucial information and warnings concerning safety issues, weather, tides, and events that may affect your enjoyment of a particular trip. Although they may sound alarmist, safety should be foremost in your mind.

4. Palm trees and beach at a Keys campground

You're in a very little boat in a very large body of water, often far from shore. You'll enjoy your trip best if you're fully informed and confident of your abilities.

Tidal Differences

The times of high and low tide vary widely along the backcountry and oceanfront waters of the Florida Keys. This applies to some areas that are just a few miles apart. Perky Creek, just fifteen miles north of Key West, has high tide five and a half hours later than Key West; the low tide at Perky Creek is nearly eight and a half hours later. Similarly, a backcountry destination near a certain mile marker on U.S. 1 can experience high tide at a different time than a destination near the same mile marker on the ocean side.

Calculating the tidal differences for launch sites and destinations is especially important for areas where tidal creeks and channels sweep huge amounts of water through small areas at a rapid rate. These areas include the Content, Snipe, Mud, and Lower Harbor Keys. Tidal differences are also particularly critical for areas surrounded by shoals and sandbars, which can be impassable during low (skinny) water. Among these areas are Bottle Key, Big Torch, Summerland Key, Saddlebunch Bay, and Similar Sound.

Always consult a daily tide table and make tidal difference calculations (using table 1 on pages 30–31) before taking a trip.

Icons

All of the trips described here should provide enjoyable "time on the water." Some also offer exceptional opportunities to visit historical sites, view wildlife, explore coral patch reefs, swim, or watch the sunset. Icons mark these special-interest trips. Trips that are especially kid-friendly also have icons, as do those that are suitable for canoeists. Other icons indicate trips where kayaks can be rented and where state or national parks offer camping facilities or ferry service.

Ferry   Kayak Rentals   Canoe OK   Camping   Snorkeling   Historical

Wildlife Viewing   Fishing   Kid Friendly   Swimming   Sunset Spot

Table 2. Launch Sites for Florida Keys Kayak Trips (by Mile Marker)

Mile Marker	Trip Name
SW 328th St. (Homestead)	Biscayne National Park: Elliott Key to Boca Chita Key—Overnight Camp
SW 328th St. (Homestead)	Biscayne National Park: Elliott Key to Old Rhodes Key—Overnight Camp
MM 111	Everglades National Park: Flagler Railroad Ruins
MM 104.5	Dusenbury Creek: In Search of the Elusive Manatee
MM 102.5	John Pennekamp State Park Canoe Trail
MM 92	Bottle Key: Roseate Spoonbill Habitat
MM 79	Inside and around Shell Key
MM 77.5	Lignumvitae Key: Trip to a Virgin Tropical Forest and Historic Homestead
MM 77.8	A Paddle and Tour of Indian Key
MM 77.8	The Wreck of the *San Pedro*
MM 71	Long Key Bight and Beach
MM 67.5	Long Key State Park Canoe Trail

Table 2—*Continued*

Mile Marker	Trip Name
MM 56.1	Curry Hammock State Park: A Paddle off Fat Deer Key
MM 50.2	Sisters Creek
MM 39.9	(Better than) Money Keys
MM 38.9	Circumnavigating Bahia Honda Key
MM 30.5	No Name Key: Around the Key Deer's Forest
MM 30.5	Exploring the Tidal Creeks of Cutoe Key
MM 28.3	Snorkeling Patch Reefs off the Newfound Harbor Keys
MM 27.9	Getting Lost in the Torches
MM 27.9	Out to the Content Keys
MM 25	Circumnavigating Toptree Hammock Key
MM 25	Circumnavigating Little Knockemdown Key
MM 21.5	The Bay on Knockemdown Key
MM 21.5	Birding through the Budd Keys to Hurricane Key
MM 21.5	Tarpon Belly Key and the Little Swash Keys
MM 21.5	Riding Key and Sawyer Key
MM 17	Perky Creek
MM 17	Up and around Upper Sugarloaf Sound
MM 16	Five Mile Creek
MM 16	Sugarloaf Creek
MM 16	Patch Reef Bonanza Shuttle Trip: Sugarloaf Key to Geiger Key
MM 11	Skinny-Water Kayaking in the Saddlebunches
MM 10.8	Similar Sound
MM 10.8	Saddlebunch Bay
MM 10.8	Geiger Coral Heads
MM 10.8	West Washerwoman Reef
MM 10.8	Geiger Creek
MM 10.8	Circumnavigating Geiger Key
MM 10	Halfmoon Key
MM 10	Duck Key and Fish Hawk Key
MM 10	Tidal Creeks of the Northern Snipe Keys and Snipe Point Beach
MM 10	Mud Keys
MM 6	Channel Key
MM 4.1	Around and through Cayo Agua
MM 4.1	Lower Harbor Keys
MM 1	Key West Beaches and Coral Heads
MM 1	Just West of Key West
70 nautical miles west of Key West	Dry Tortugas National Park: Day Trip Dry Tortugas National Park: Overnight Camp

Trip # 1

Biscayne National Park: Elliott Key to Boca Chita Key—Overnight Camp

Launch Site: SW 328th Street, Homestead, Florida (on the mainland north of Key Largo)

Location: Biscayne National Park (40-minute park service concessionaire boat ride to Elliott Key, 40-minute return trip)

Paddling Time: 4 hours (after taking ferry to Elliott Key)

Comments: Overnight camping on an island at the northern tip of the Florida Keys. Paddling through protected shallow waters with rich opportunities for snorkeling, swimming, and fishing. Ornamental lighthouse.

Note: A trip to Biscayne National Park takes advance planning. Although it is possible to paddle the eight nautical miles across Biscayne Bay to Elliott Key, you may want to pay a park service concessionaire to transport you and your boat to the campground. This will save you time and energy which you can better use to explore the shallow waters near shore, and you'll get a chance to snorkel the main fringe reef as well. Round-trip passage to Elliott Key costs $25/person plus $16/kayak, and is offered only from November through May. Reservations are recommended. Before stopping at Elliott Key the boat goes out to the offshore reef for a one-hour snorkel trip. (There is a small additional charge for snorkeling). The boat will drop you off at the Elliott Key campground at 4 P.M. Be sure to let the captain know which day you'd like to be picked up by the snorkel boat (also at 4 P.M.). The campground on Elliott Key is popular on weekends and holidays. The campground on Boca Chita Key is more primitive—no drinking water, showers, or ranger on duty. It is very crowded on weekends. Camping is first-come-first-served, and a $10/night fee is charged. Mosquitoes can be thick on the islands! Be forewarned.

To reach Elliott Key you'll first need to drive to Biscayne National Park's Dante Fascell Visitor Center in Homestead, Florida. It's located at the end of 328th Street, which intersects with U.S. 1 in Homestead (328th

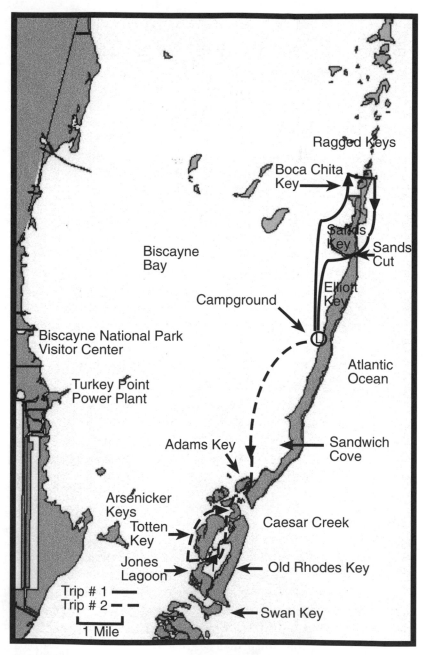

Ragged Keys

Boca Chita Key

Biscayne Bay

Sands Key

Sands Cut

Elliott Key

Campground

Biscayne National Park Visitor Center

Atlantic Ocean

Turkey Point Power Plant

Adams Key

Sandwich Cove

Arsenicker Keys

Totten Key

Caesar Creek

Jones Lagoon

Old Rhodes Key

Trip # 1 ——
Trip # 2 - - -

1 Mile

Swan Key

3.1. Biscayne National Park: Trips # 1–2

Street can also be reached via the Florida Turnpike by exiting at Speedway Boulevard—SW 137th Avenue—south, then following signs for the park). The visitor center features exhibits on the area's natural history, has a small bookstore which sells nautical charts and guidebooks, and gives out free brochures with good maps of the keys and surrounding waters. The park's boat concessionaire, Biscayne National Underwater Park, Inc., is also located here. Their boat to Elliott Key leaves the dock from November through May at 12:30 P.M. After crossing Biscayne Bay it heads to one of several excellent snorkeling spots on the main fringe reef—a bonus for kayakers who otherwise must stay closer to shore. On its return trip the boat stops at Elliott Key campground at 4 P.M.

If you plan on paddling out to Elliott Key yourself, check the weather and tidal conditions at the visitor center before launching from the dock. Allow yourself approximately four hours of continuous paddling to make the passage in a sit-upon kayak. Your route will take you due east across busy Biscayne Bay to the dock at Elliott Key Harbor, marked by a twenty-five-foot flagpole and a two-story visitor center adjacent to the campground.

A trip to Boca Chita Key takes two hours each way from Elliott Key Harbor. So if you arrive on Elliott Key late in the afternoon you'll have two choices—setting up camp there and visiting Boca Chita the next day or heading straight for Boca Chita. Whatever your decision, you'll leave from Elliott Key Harbor. Launch your kayak from the harbor and head right (north) up the bayside of Elliott Key en route to Sands Key. The water here is quite shallow near shore and while there can be many powerboats in the park, especially on weekends, they tend to stay in the deeper waters of Biscayne Bay until they reach Sands Key. It will take you a little over one hour to reach the southern shore of Sands Key. Because this is a no-wake zone, it is a good spot to rest and take in the scenery.

Another hour's paddle will take you up the western shore of Sands Key and across Lewis Cut to Boca Chita Key. Be on the lookout for power-boaters coming through the channel on your left. They'll likely have their eyes set on the lighthouse and harbor, not on your kayak. Unless you're camping, you may want to pull your boat ashore on the sandy beach before the harbor. This way you can walk to the lighthouse and avoid the powerboaters. The view from the lighthouse offers another perspective

Most people consider Key Largo to be the first bit of land in the Florida Keys island chain. It is, after all, the first one that you can reach by car. But the Keys actually start farther north in the waters of Biscayne Bay, and to reach them you must travel by water.

That's how the Tequesta Indians, who were the Keys' first inhabitants, did it. That's how Ponce de Leon reached these keys in 1513 while searching for the Fountain of Youth. Bahamian mahogany tree-cutters arrived by boat, as did Black Caesar the pirate and early pineapple and lime farmers. Rumrunners darted in and out of the islands during Prohibition. Everyone, in fact, arrived by one sort of boat or another, and until the 1920s this didn't seem to bother anyone in South Florida.

Then in 1929 horticulturist Dr. John Gifford, a famous champion of draining the Everglades, became the first to advocate joining the northern Keys to the mainland by means of a causeway. Nothing came of his plan until 1960, when real estate developers and Dade County politicians joined together to plan an upscale community on Elliott Key, dubbed Islandia. One of their marketing claims was that residents would be able to reach their new homes by a causeway bridge over Biscayne Bay. This, they thought, would make it an easy sell. But the developers didn't anticipate opposition to their plans, and they were unprepared for the strong public disapproval that ensued. Criticism of both the development and the bridge, coupled with misconceived plans for an oil refinery, dump, and nuclear power plant in the vicinity, eventually led to the creation of a highly organized, well-financed conservation movement. Public pressure and heavy lobbying led to Congressional designation of Biscayne National Monument less than eight months after developers began bulldozing 120-foot-wide Elliott Key Boulevard. Instead of accelerating residential development in the area, the Islandia project brought an end to it. Within twenty years Biscayne National Monument was enlarged to its present size (181,500 acres, 95 percent of which is water) and declared a national park.

The abandoned Islandia roadbed on Elliott Key is now a self-guided hiking trail. The island hosts a national park campground with picnic tables, grills, rest rooms, showers, and drinking water. Nearby Boca Chita Key is more spartan. It has no water at its campground and no park ranger on duty. It does, however, boast remnants of a millionaire's estate capped off with a small lighthouse on its northwestern shore. Either of the islands makes a pleasant base camp for long and short paddles.

on the spectacular scenery of Biscayne Bay as well as your first view of the Atlantic Ocean and its fringe reef.

Whether you camp overnight on Boca Chita Key or return to Elliott Key later in the day, you will probably want to circumnavigate the island by heading right (east) out of the harbor and continuing down along its oceanside before heading across Lewis Cut. This will give you beautiful views out to sea. If conditions are favorable, you could continue along the oceanside all the way to Sands Cut before heading back into the near-shore waters of Biscayne Bay for the trip to camp on Elliott Key.

FYI:

Daily boat service (November–May) to Elliott Key from Biscayne National Park Visitor Center is available from

Biscayne National Underwater Park, Inc.
9710 SW 328th Street
Homestead, FL 33033
(305) 230-1100

Additional information on the park is available from

Biscayne National Park
9700 SW 328th Street
Homestead, FL 33033-5634
(305) 230-7275
www.nps.gov/bisc

Trip # 2

Biscayne National Park: Elliott Key to Old Rhodes Key—Overnight Camp

Launch Site: SW 328th Street, Homestead, Florida (on the mainland north of Key Largo)
Location: Biscayne National Park (40-minute park service concessionaire boat ride to Elliott Key, 40-minute return trip)
Paddling Time: 6 hours (after taking the ferry)
Comments: Overnight camping on an island at the northern tip of the Florida Keys. Paddle through a group of mangrove islands to a peaceful lagoon.
Note: See note to trip # 1.

Launch your kayak from Elliott Key Harbor and head left (south) down the long length of the key. As you paddle along the mangrove shoreline you'll see herons, ibis, egrets, and pelicans bending the branches, and you'll have an unimpeded view across Biscayne Bay. It will take you about an hour to reach Sandwich Cove with its two tiny mangrove islets. From

You could easily camp on Elliott Key for a week and spend each day exploring the nearshore waters of Biscayne Bay and the Atlantic Ocean. This area is a microcosm of the Keys' varied environment, containing long stretches of shoreline, backcountry mangrove islands, shallow-water lagoons, tidal cuts and creeks, patch reefs, and sandy beaches. With a nautical chart, tide table, compass, and weather radio to guide you, the possibilities here really are endless. But because of the park's proximity to Miami, you are likely to have a fair amount of company on the water, especially of the powerboat variety. If you want to leave the noise and fumes behind, then go where powerboats can't—between Old Rhodes and Totten Key. These islands just south of Elliott Key personify "skinny water," less than a foot deep at mean low tide. Check your tide table before loading up your gear.

here it's just a thirty-minute paddle to the dock at Adams Key. There's a picnic area here, as well as rest rooms and a nature trail, but there is no fresh drinking water. Aside from being a pleasant place to stretch your legs, Adams Key has quite a story to tell. Back in the 1920s it was the site of the Cocolobo Club, an informal casino for the likes of President Warren Harding, Harvey Firestone, and the head of General Motors. The brainchild of Miami developer Carl Fisher, the Cocolobo was the birthplace of many a business deal.

Nearby Porgy Key was the home of the Parson family—Israel and Moselle and their two children, King Arthur and Prince Lancelot. These resourceful farmers and fishermen eked out a living on the key, supplementing their income by serving as bonefishing guides to the rich and famous, including several American presidents.

As you leave the dock on Adams Key, heading southwest, you'll paddle briefly across Caesar Creek, named for Black Caesar, the pirate. Watch out for strong tidal currents here. Next paddle between Reid Key on your right and Porgy Key on your left. This will keep you in shallow water away from the powerboats plying Hurricane Creek. The shoreline directly ahead of you is Totten Key. When you reach it, after about fifteen minutes of paddling, head left along its shore. This will take you between Totten on your right and Old Rhodes Key on your left. Hundreds of tiny mangrove islets fill shallow Jones Lagoon here. Named for the African-American family who homesteaded here as early as 1902, it's a haven for wading birds. Paddling straight down the lagoon, holding fast to the shore of Totten Key, takes about half an hour, although you could spend much longer exploring Old Rhodes' curving shoreline. A tiny creek separating Old Rhodes Key from Little Totten Key at the far southeastern end of the lagoon is well worth the visit if you have the time.

When you reach the southern end of Jones Lagoon, bear right around the tip of Totten Key. Within fifteen minutes you'll spot tiny Crane Creek on your right, the last sheltered spot before heading north up the bayside shoreline of Totten Key. Once at Totten's northern end, retrace your route between Porgy and Reid Keys and across busy Caesar Creek. You may want to stretch again and hit the bathrooms on Adams Key before the two-hour paddle back to your campsite on Elliott Key.

FYI:

Same as for trip # 1

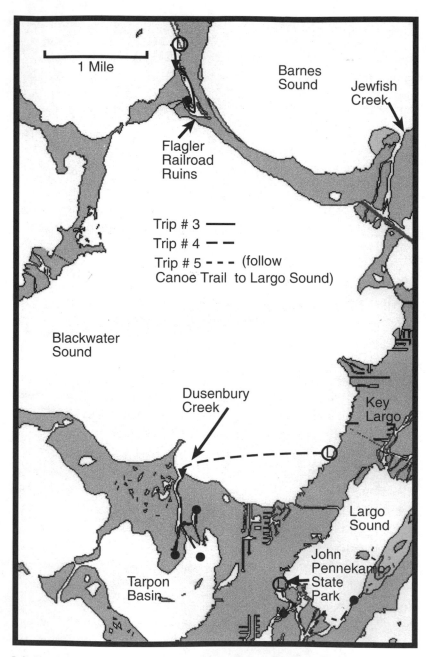

1 Mile

Barnes
Sound

Jewfish
Creek

Flagler
Railroad
Ruins

Trip # 3 ——
Trip # 4 — —
Trip # 5 - - - (follow
Canoe Trail to Largo Sound)

Blackwater
Sound

Dusenbury
Creek

Key
Largo

Largo
Sound

John
Pennekamp
State
Park

Tarpon
Basin

3.2. Key Largo: Trips # 3–5

Trip # 3

Everglades National Park: Flagler Railroad Ruins

Launch Site: MM 111 (bayside)
Location: Everglades National Park, off the 18-mile stretch of U.S. 1 north of Key Largo
Paddling Time: 45 minutes
Comments: Nice, easy paddle that's well suited to beginning kayakers. Historical interest.
Note: No fishing allowed, owing to mercury poisoning.

Florida Keys roads officially begin just outside Florida City with a section of U.S. 1 known to locals as "the eighteen-mile stretch." This dangerous two-lane road is a sort of extended speed-bump connecting the U.S. mainland, especially Miami, to the hundred-mile Keys archipelago. If there is ever a toll road to Cuba, it will probably have the same gestalt.

As you drive south, on your left you see stands of red mangrove and Biscayne Bay. On your right you can see the Crocodile Refuge section of Everglades National Park. The water on your left is oceanic, on your right brackish. Both offer great kayaking opportunities. Pay close attention to the green mile-marker signs. Traffic here can be thick and fast, so you'll want to have plenty of time to signal your turn onto the launch site. At MM 111 there is a boat launch on the Florida Bay side. Pull off here and unload your gear, then park your car away from the launch. (Park only on the shell apron beside the road. If that area is full, drive on. It is unsafe and illegal to park in any other area.)

Once you're in your boat, head left (south) through a small mangrove channel which soon opens onto a lake tucked along the eastern shore of Little Blackwater Sound.

Imagine yourself in a leather-appointed, table-linened club car on the Overseas Railroad. The year is 1912, and you are among the first to travel on Henry Flagler's eighth wonder of the world. Flagler became a millionaire in the early twentieth century as CEO of the Standard Oil Company. As a follow-up to that career he dedicated himself to pursuing his dream—to construct what he called "the railroad that went to sea." His stated aim was to extend the route of his successful East Coast trains to Key West, where they would link up with freight and passenger ships from Cuba and the Caribbean. To many it must have seemed that he wanted to walk on water and enable others to do so.

His railroad ended up taking seven years and several million dollars to build. Thirty thousand men worked on the project, and 170 died. Three deadly hurricanes menaced the workers. Then, twenty-three years after the railroad's completion, the Labor Day Hurricane of 1935 took eight hundred lives and utterly destroyed the Overseas Railroad's tracks, supplies, tenders' houses, and locomotives. Still, for those like American novelist John Dos Passos, who wrote Ernest Hemingway about his "dreamlike journey" on a rail trip to Key West, the view (at fifteen miles an hour) from above one of the trestled bridges must have been magnificent.

The remnants of the Overseas Railroad's trestles march two by two from key to mangrovey key in the little lake ahead of you. They are all that is left of what some called Flagler's Folly. As you paddle by them, be cautious—occasionally pilings are submerged and could easily tip over your kayak. Take time to appreciate the natural beauty of this area and the bird life that frequents it. Then picture yourself in Key West on January 12, 1912, as Henry Flagler's train pulls into town on its inaugural run. A brass band and flag-waving schoolchildren are on hand to provide the proper small-town Victorian fanfare. Henry Flagler is smiling. Already he is planning his next feat—taking his rail cars all the way to Cuba.

Trip # 4

Dusenbury Creek: In Search of the Elusive Manatee

Launch Site: MM 104.5 (bayside)
Location: Dusenbury Creek, Key Largo
Paddling Time: 2½ hours
Comments: Quiet mangrove habitat frequented by manatees during winter and early spring.
Note: Kayak rentals available. Boat traffic in Blackwater Sound and Dusenbury Creek can be intimidating.

The west coast of Florida is probably the best-known habitat of the remarkable West Indian manatee. A cottage industry of sorts has sprung up there in recent years as tourists flock to see, photograph, and (increasingly) snorkel with these odd-looking, somewhat elephantine sea mammals. Manatees are also found in the Keys, especially in the mangrove creeks and seagrass meadows of the Upper Keys. At three thousand pounds and thirteen feet, you would think they'd be hard to miss, but these "sea cows" have adapted their dull gray coloration to match their submarine environment. This, combined with their shyness, has made them somewhat hard to spot in their natural habitat. In fact, manatees are becoming victims of such camouflage. Historically these herbivores have favored tidal creeks and seagrass meadows for their grazing. They are slow-moving mammals that stay submerged for five to twenty minutes between surface breaths, rising unexpectedly from the dark water. Today motorboaters kill nearly a hundred manatees a year and scar hundreds of others' thick hides by running over the sea cows with their propellers. Last year 268 manatees died, out of a total population of 3,000, despite the fact that they have been protected since the 1970s by both the Endangered Species Act and the Marine Mammal Protection Act.

The launch site for this trip is on the bayside of Key Largo at Florida Bay Outfitters. This helpful kayak and canoe center sells and rents boats, conducts kayak trips, and has laminated nautical charts of the nearshore bay and ocean waters annotated with good birding spots and other features. They will let you park and launch from their site.

Look around you as you enter the water. Shoreline development in Key Largo can be bewildering, so it's best to make a mental note of key landmarks which you can look for on the return leg of your trip.

Once on the water, head to your left, bearing northwest for the promontory of Bush Point. Watch for boat traffic, which can be thick in this area. In about half an hour you'll see a channel marker as Dusenbury Creek opens up below Bush Point. This is part of the Intracoastal Waterway and is heavily traveled. Stay to the right side of the channel and keep an eye out for the wake of passing boats and Jet Skis. Within fifteen minutes you'll be able to pass to your right at a no-wake sign and enter the first of several quiet mangrove creeks that are too shallow for most powerboats. The water becomes clearer as you paddle another ten minutes and enter a lovely small lagoon. At its terminus lie two smaller creeks, one on the left, one on the right. Entering these will probably make you feel like Alice in her Looking Glass world—you will feel small indeed in your little boat as you look up to the roof of the mangrove tunnel which nearly obliterates the sky. Trilling insects fill the air, while green baitfish flash in the filtered sunlight below your boat.

The surest way to see a manatee may be to visit the manatee pool at Homosassa Springs Wildlife State Park north of Tampa, but a more interesting way is to venture into the mangrove tunnels off Dusenbury Creek in your kayak. To spot a sea cow, it's best to take your trip during the winter months either early in the morning or late in the day. If you do see a manatee, you will be certain that your boat can't injure it, and you'll be able to observe it undisturbed—hearing its massive breath, watching as its round paddle-shaped tail slips back under water. If you don't see a manatee, you can still enjoy the dense canopy of the beautiful mangrove tunnels. Herons and ibis will likely rise up from their roosts as you paddle alongside them. The filtered sunlight may highlight a brightly colored endangered tree snail. There's no telling what you'll find.

Retrace your route and, if you wish, cross Dusenbury Creek to a small creek directly opposite you. It opens up onto a sunny lagoon. There is also another small creek to explore. Keep an eye out for manatees as you paddle, and stay awhile in the calm waters before heading back through busy Dusenbury Creek. As you emerge from the creek, scan the shoreline, adjusting your course as the bridge of the Marvin D. Adams Waterway comes into view. Proceed along the shoreline to the launch site.

Whether or not you see any manatees, you'll learn more about their once pristine habitat and the challenges they now face. Once mistaken for mermaids, these gentle sea mammals' future is uncertain. They'll need all the friends they can get.

FYI:

You can find out more about manatees and how to help save them by contacting:

Save the Manatee Club, Maitland, Florida

Sierra Club

Florida Audubon Society

Defenders of Wildlife

Humane Society of the United States

Florida Marine Patrol

Trip # 5

John Pennekamp State Park Canoe Trail

Launch Site: MM 102.5 (oceanside)
Location: John Pennekamp Coral Reef State Park, Key Largo
Paddling Time: 1 to 1½ hours
Comments: Well-marked, easy paddle along a signed canoe trail in a popular state park.
Note: Kayak rentals and camping available. Reservations recommended.

Founded in 1960 as the first undersea park in the United States, John Pennekamp Coral Reef State Park is also Florida's most popular state park—at least as gauged by the number of annual visitors. It is close enough to the Miami metropolitan area to be a convenient getaway spot, but it attracts visitors from all over the country and the world because of the coral reef that lies just offshore. Concessionaires take snorkelers and divers to the reef and rent plenty of powerboats, too. A gentler way to explore the area is by kayak, and you can either bring your own or rent one by the hour or day. With more than 178 nautical miles of coral reefs, seagrass beds, and mangrove habitat, there is plenty to explore. And while you cannot reach the fringe reefs by kayak, you can paddle through the mangrove and beach areas of the park. Then, if you wish, you can join a reef trip or take a ride in a glass-bottomed boat.

A good introduction to the park can be had in the visitor center, open daily from 8 A.M. to 5 P.M. Natural history exhibits depict the park's three main ecosystems, a theater and rangers provide additional information, and a thirty-thousand-gallon saltwater aquarium lets you see what will likely be swimming under your hull.

To reach the Canoe Trail launch site, consult the map you're given at the park's front gate. Proceed south past the marina and the dump station to the Campfire Circle, where you can park and unload your gear. There are picnic tables here, too, for before- or after-paddle meals.

Push off toward your right. For a short distance you'll be in the main boat channel, so keep an eye out for novice powerboaters and charter boats full of sunburned snorkelers. Soon you will see a Canoe Trail sign, which you should follow, keeping to the right side of the channel. You can relax now as you watch snappers and schools of baitfish weave in and out of the luxurious seagrass unfurling beneath your boat. Watch for herons, egrets, and ibis roosting in the mangroves that line this creek. Eventually the creek widens and reaches a large channel marked with a prominent canoe sign with a broad stroke through it. This is not so much an eviction notice as a warning—from that point on, expect powerboaters and Jet Skis to rush through South Sound Creek en route to the blue water out front. Let them go. Retrace your route to where you first saw the Canoe Trail sign, this time heading in the opposite direction (you will have been on the water about half an hour). Soon you'll come across an observation deck, which you can moor up to if you like. A tower there provides a nice spot for bird-watching. Back in your kayak, you can paddle another fifteen minutes or so through the lush creek before it empties into Largo Sound.

Two channel markers (20 and 21) point powerboaters to this relatively deep channel, but the waters just ahead on the southern edge of Largo Sound are less than a foot deep and make for great quiet paddling. You can explore three small mangrove islets or cruise the shoreline of El Radabob Key. The hardbottom seafloor here hosts beautiful sea sponges, and you're likely to see sharks as well.

From the eastern edge of Largo Sound it's possible to enter North Sound Creek. An area just south of that creek, between Sound Point and

---

Don't Touch the Coral!

John Pennekamp Coral Reef State Park is named for a Miami newspaper editor who understood the need to protect this fragile ecosystem long before his contemporaries did. When U.S. Navy engineers completed an eighteen-inch water pipeline from Florida City to Key West in 1942, tourists and "freshwater Conchs" (new year-round residents) poured into the Keys. Enterprising '50s businessmen used crowbars and dynamite to harvest coral trinkets from the reef for roadside sale to the newcomers.

The establishment of John Pennekamp State Park marked a legal end to the plunder, but even today the sight of an enthusiastic snorkeler triumphantly carrying a prized sea fan "souvenir" up from the seafloor is far too common.

Coral is living matter. Touching it kills it. Standing on it kills it. Flicking it with your flipper kills it. It has taken billions of marine organisms nearly seven thousand years to create the reefs that fringe the Keys. Do your part to protect this national natural monument.

Rattlesnake Key, is a good bird-watching site. This trip would add several hours to your paddling time and require either a nautical chart or one of the laminated Key Largo charts available from Florida Bay Outfitters (see trip # 4). Whatever your route, keep an eye out for powerboaters and Jet Skis on the return leg of your trip.

It'd be nice to stop and let a ranger know how much you enjoyed your nonmotorized trip and encourage them to provide more opportunities for paddlers.

FYI:

Forty-seven campsites, for tents and RVs, can be reserved up to eleven months in advance by calling (800) 326-3521. Boat rentals, snorkeling and scuba trips, and other concessions can also be arranged in advance. Additional information on the park is available from

John Pennekamp Coral Reef State Park
P.O. Box 1560
Key Largo, FL 33037
www.dep.state.fl.us/parks

Trip # 6

Bottle Key: Roseate Spoonbill Habitat

Launch Site: MM 92 (bayside) to Jo-Jean Way
Location: Bottle Key, a mangrove island in Florida Bay, due north of Tavernier
Paddling Time: 4 hours
Comments: Open-water journey with chances to see rare roseate spoonbills in season (November–April).
Note: Be careful if you take this trip at or near low tide. The key is surrounded by banks and shallows on both sides, and the marly seafloor makes for mucky portaging. Also be very careful not to disturb nesting birds.

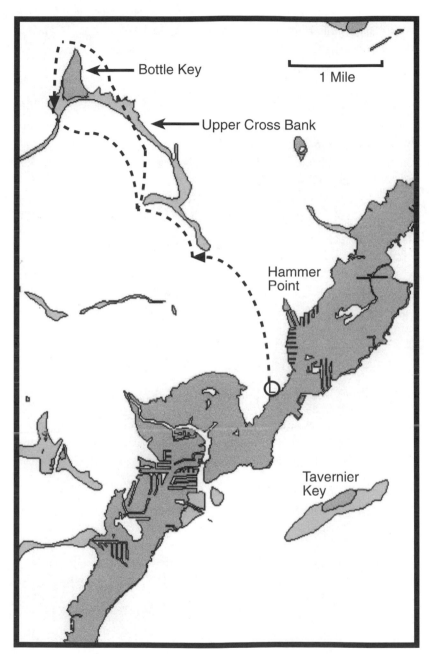

1 Mile

Bottle Key

Upper Cross Bank

Hammer
Point

Tavernier
Key

3.3. Bottle Key: Trip # 6

"Flame birds" is the name that ornithologist Robert Porter Allen gave the roseate spoonbills he studied on Bottle Key in 1939 and 1940. Having seen them, I can't think of a better nickname. Roseate spoonbills are wading birds less than three feet high, members of the ibis family. When standing in the marly flats of Florida Bay, they appear to be all legs and neck, their long gray bills terminating in an indisputable spoon. But when roosting, set against a backdrop of dark green mangrove leaves, or flying through a deeply azure sky, their colors come alive—a gentle pale pink on their back and belly, brilliant fuchsia wings, and a short orangish tail, all illuminated by the tropical sun.

We are lucky that these incredible birds still exist. Plume hunters in the early 1900s reduced the once flourishing Florida population to a single breeding pair nesting on Bottle Key in 1939. Captivated by their color and soft plumage, Victorian ladies took to accessorizing themselves with roseate fans consisting of a whole wing torn off a bird and attached to a paddle. I've seen just such a fan in an antique clothing store. It was pale and threadbare and cost $75.

To reach the launch site, take U.S. 1 to MM 92 and then turn onto Jo-Jean Way, a short road that leads to a public boat launch on Florida Bay. This is a residential area, so be sure to park in a designated area after unloading your gear. As you push off past a few nearshore mangroves, take note of your surroundings. The large white condo behind you will make a good reference point on your return, as will the Eiffel Tower–looking an-

To see a live roseate spoonbill you can visit J. N. "Ding" Darling National Wildlife Refuge at Sanibel Island on Florida's west coast or keep your fingers crossed on a morning hike through the mangroves of the Keys. A kayak trip to the islands of Florida Bay in the winter nesting season will give you a chance not only of seeing spoonbills but of knowing their habitat firsthand. Nesting spoonbills frequent several islands off Key Largo. A beautiful paddle to Bottle Key may provide spoonbill sightings, and you can compare your experience with those of Robert Porter Allen, who documented his year-and-a-half ornithological study in *The Flame Birds*.

tennae farther back and some distinctive houses to your right. As you clear the mangroves you will see Bottle Key due north of you, surrounded by shallows and banks.

You can paddle directly to Bottle Key or take a more luxurious approach, as I do, paddling for forty-five minutes or so to Upper Cross Bank southeast of the island. Here at low tide you'll find milky aquamarine waters dotted with mangrove seedlings, a nice respite from the powerboaters plying the deeper channels. Wading birds are a common sight here, and you might be lucky enough to see a spoonbill waving its bill from side to side as it scoops aquatic invertebrates from the mud. You are now within the boundaries of Everglades National Park, and you'll likely be welcomed by anhingas, the emblematic black diving birds of the area. They hold their wings out to dry, lacking the oil glands of other waterfowl, and sometimes look like scarecrows improbably plopped down in the sea. Behind you, stretching up the length of Key Largo, are hundreds of gleaming white condos, hotels, and stores; to the west lie mile upon mile of mangroves, filtering nearshore waters through their prop roots, sheltering young fish and crustaceans.

Leaving this bank, you'll paddle northwest through several islets before making a skinny-water passage into the harbor on Bottle Key's east side (if you've spent a little time on Upper Cross Bank, you will have been gone about an hour and a half since launching). This is a good anchorage with a nice small beach, so don't be surprised if you're joined by a sailboat. Remember to keep your distance from any islands in this area during nesting season so as not to disturb the birds that might be there. Eggs can be destroyed quickly by the tropical sun if the parents are spooked from their nest.

By paddling north, then west out of the harbor you can circumnavigate the island. From here you can also see, two miles to the north, three small islands named the Bob Keys for the spoonbills' chronicler, Robert Allen. There is excellent fishing in Bottle Key Bank off the island's western shore, and more farther south on Ramshorn Shoal. But just paddling is fine, too, with sharks and rays gliding through the water and amazing vistas on all sides.

As you catch sight of the antennae tower and head back to shore, savor the seascape around you and be thankful that bright pink and orange birds somehow defied the odds, escaped the poachers, and still swing their spoon-shaped bills back and forth in the thousand-shaded blue water of the Florida Keys.

Trip # 7

Inside and around Shell Key

Launch Site: MM 79 (bayside)
Location: Shell Key, a mangrove island in Florida Bay north of Upper Matecumbe Key
Paddling Time: 2 to 2¼ hours
Comments: Circumnavigation of a key with a rare chance to paddle inside it to a small lagoon.
Note: Remain in your boat when exploring the interior. Because this is a bird sanctuary, it is illegal to go ashore. Kayak rentals available at MM 77.5 (Florida Keys Kayak & Sail).

While it's true that "the map is not the territory," some maps are so intriguing that they propel us to firsthand exploration. The cartographic profile of Shell Key got me wondering—what would it look like inside the donut hole of this mangrove island? Could it, in fact, be reached by boat? I got my answer from one of the park rangers at nearby Lignumvitae Key. After a walk through the hardwood hammock there, I asked her if she'd ever been to Shell Key and if it was possible to reach its interior lagoon. She gave me directions, which I pass on here, along with her warning that this is vitally important habitat for birds and other creatures—so vital that people are banned from setting foot on the island. So go there in your kayak, leave only bubbles, and enjoy the view.

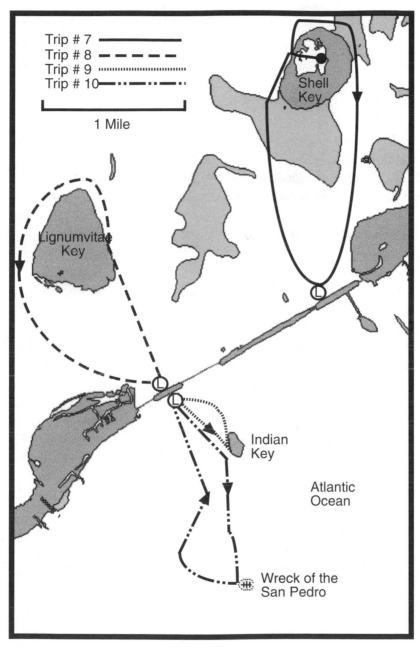

Trip # 7 ——————
Trip # 8 ― ― ― ―
Trip # 9 ··············
Trip # 10 —··—··—··—

1 Mile

Shell
Key

Lignumvitae
Key

Indian
Key

Atlantic
Ocean

Wreck of the
San Pedro

3.4. Matecumbe Keys Area: Trips # 7–10

To reach the launch site, pull off U.S. 1 on the bayside at MM 79 near Teatable Bridge. There is plenty of parking here. You'll see Shell Key due north of the launch site, just across the channel from Lignumvitae Key, which has a discernible boat dock on its eastern shore. Align your kayak with Shell Key's western shore and push off, mindful of the boats that rip through Teatable Channel (often scarring the seagrass meadows that lie beneath these shallow waters). By keeping to the shallower water you'll avoid the sometimes frenzied powerboaters and have a better chance of spotting southern rays, sharks, and leaping schools of baitfish. It will take you about half an hour to reach the southwestern shore of Shell Key.

As you paddle along this shore you'll see mooring buoys and a sign that welcomes people to Shell Key Preserve (reminding them not to trespass on the island). Then half an hour later you'll see a second sign. A very low, narrow mangrove tunnel lies just to the left of this sign. Enter it cautiously: it is very narrow and overhung with branches. Next to your ear you're likely to see a tree crab climbing up a mangrove. Underneath your boat, juvenile snappers school. The humming of insects fills the air, along with the twittering of birds. After five minutes you'll enter a small sunlit lagoon pulsating with thousands of celadon green upside-down jellyfish. These jellyfish are mildly toxic, causing itching and then a rash. Don't scoop them up, but do admire the way their eight long oral arms sway in the current. They are feeding, using a mouth that is divided into several tiny pores along these oral arms. Strange and beautiful, with lettucelike filaments, together they look like a sea garden full of flowers continually blooming. Their Latin name is *Cassiopeia*, the same as that of a beautiful constellation of stars.

After retracing your route through the tiny mangrove tunnel you can proceed north and east on a circumnavigation of the key. Shell Key Flat, off the island's northeastern shore, is an excellent fishing ground. Mangroves poke up through the shallow waters here, and wading birds are a common sight, especially toward sunset. When you're ready to head back to Upper Matecumbe, align yourself with the patch of land to the right of the transmitter tower, keeping to the left-hand side of Teatable Channel. The hum of the highway will draw you back to your car.

Trip # 8

Lignumvitae Key: Trip to a Virgin Tropical Forest and Historic Homestead

Launch Site: MM 77.5 (bayside)
Location: Lignumvitae Key, between Upper and Lower Matecumbe Keys
Paddling Time: 1 hour round-trip to the key, 1 hour more to circumnavigate it
Comments: Popular trip to a state botanical site with rare orchids, tree cacti, hardwood hammock, and historic homestead. Best time to visit is April, when the lignum vitae tree is in bloom.
Note: Kayak rentals available from Florida Keys Kayak & Sail, behind the Hungry Tarpon Restaurant. The park is closed on Tuesdays and Wednesdays and daily from sundown to 8 A.M. Ranger-led tours at 10 A.M. and 2 P.M., $1 fee. Mosquitoes can be brutal onshore. (To its credit, the state doesn't allow pesticide spraying on this key; to the insects' credit, they know a good meal when they see one.) Be forewarned.

Lignumvitae Key is named for a remarkable tropical hardwood found in the Florida Keys and parts of the Caribbean. Known as "holy wood" and often cited as the mythical tree in the Garden of Eden whose wood was used to fashion the Holy Grail and impart immortality, lignum vitae means "wood of life" in Latin. Used for centuries to treat syphilis, arthritis, tonsillitis, gout, rheumatism, and other diseases, it was considered the penicillin of its day. It is also one of the hardest and densest woods in the world, and has a grain so interlaced that it's nearly impossible to split. Fully 30 percent of its weight comes from its resin, making the wood self-lubricating. This has made lignum vitae indispensable in the manufacture of submarine propeller shafts and machinery bearings and for other military and industrial uses. A victim of its own success, slow-growing lignum vitae has been harvested to near extinction in many areas and is found in the United States only in the Florida Keys.

The tree and its flowers are beautiful. Diminutive in stature, reaching twenty-five feet in height and a foot and a half feet in diameter, it is an evergreen with dark green leaves and deep purplish blue star-shaped flowers which bloom in March and April. Small green fruits turn gold in the fall, splitting open to reveal bright red seeds.

To reach Lignumvitae Key, pull off U.S. 1 at MM 77.5 and launch from the roadside park on the bayside of the highway. Lignumvitae is the large key due north on the west (left) side of Lignumvitae Channel. As you paddle through the shallow seagrass beds here, it's impossible to ignore the many boat prop scars that gouge the seafloor. With seagrass meadows

---

Lignum vitae are the stars of the virgin tropical hardwood hammock protected by this botanical state park, but other exotic trees and plants are also worth examining. Park rangers conduct two one-hour tours of the hammock, starting from Matheson House at 10 A.M. and 2 P.M. Their knowledge is invaluable. Poisonwood and manchineel, among the most toxic trees in the world, grow here. Watch closely as a ranger points them out. Strangler figs' intertwining roots create interesting sculptures as they ensnare rocks, trees, and buildings. Then there's gumbo-limbo, often called "the tourist tree" because of its bark's tendency to peel. Rare night-blooming tree cacti can be spotted in the hammock, as can *Encyclia tampense* orchids, which reward visitors in the hot and buggy months of June and July with their fragrant blossoms.

The Matheson family cleared a small section of this forest when they built their home here in 1919. It's a lovely structure, built of Dade County pine and furnished with its original chairs, tables, beds, and kitchen utensils. Built to last, it has withstood three major hurricanes. When it lost its roof in the devastating Labor Day Hurricane of 1935 (which killed hundreds on nearby Upper Matecumbe Key), the house was fitted with steel rods that run vertically through each room, tying roof to ceiling to floor to coral bedrock. In 1960 Hurricane Dora raked the island with 187-mile-an-hour winds, yet the house stood firm. And although Hurricane Georges felled many trees in the hammock in 1998, the house came through just fine.

taking up to ten years to regenerate, and with fines of several thousand dollars now being levied against irresponsible boaters, paddling a kayak here is the best ecological and economic choice. Besides, it's a nice short paddle to Lignumvitae, taking less than half an hour.

As you ply these waters, look for the yellow stingrays that frequent this area. Then head for the eastern shore of the island. You will see a high boat dock used by private boaters and tour boats from local marinas. Use the park rangers' service landing to the left of the dock instead, pulling your kayak onto the beach. (Let a ranger know you've done this; you may have to move your boat.) Bring any personal valuables with you, including an expensive paddle if you have one. Theft is highly unlikely, but the park isn't responsible for stolen items.

Extending your trip by circumnavigating this three-hundred-acre island is a nice way to admire the towering trees that line its eastern and northern shores. It's a beautiful green gem set in a turquoise sea—"the real Florida," as state park brochures put it.

FYI:

Additional information on the park can be obtained from

Lignumvitae Key Botanical State Park
P.O. Box 1052
Islamorada, FL 33036
(305) 664-2540
www.dep.state.fl.us/parks

Trip # 9

A Paddle and Tour of Indian Key

Launch Site: MM 77.8 (oceanside)
Location: Indian Key Historic State Park, just off Lower Matecumbe Key
Paddling Time: 45 minutes
Comments: Popular trip to a beautiful key with a rich history (and prehistory).

Before the tourists, before American settlers or Bahamian turtlers or Spanish sailors, Native American Indians lived for thousands of years on the sparse islands of the Florida Keys. Few artifacts remain from this prehistoric period. Historical records of the Calusa Indians do exist. They were living on Indian Key during the 1500s, when Ponce de Leon recommended that Spanish galleons start using the Florida Straits as a shortcut home from their Mexican and South American colonies. "Calusa" meant "fierce people" in the natives' language, and it was an apt name. It was a Calusa arrow, after all, which eventually killed Ponce de Leon in 1521.

This powerful culture exacted tribute from towns and villages near its capital, Calos, preserved today as Mound Key Archaeological State Park near Estero in southwest Florida. But Calusa warriors soon also learned the value of the cargo being transported by the conquistadors, and when Spanish ships foundered on the treacherous reef less than six miles from Indian Key, the Calusas salvaged it and traded it back to the Europeans in Florida and Cuba. This commerce with Europeans eventually proved fatal for the Calusa, as they succumbed to diseases to which they had no immunity. Those who survived migrated to Cuba.

Real profiteering had to wait until pirates and Bahamian fishermen and turtlers who had crossed the Gulf Stream began to salvage wrecks in the Keys. For years they scooped fortunes from the reef. Then in 1821 Spain ceded Florida to the United States. The Americans drove out both the pirates and the Bahamians, granting a monopoly to

Note: Kayak rentals available at MM 77.5. The park is closed from sundown to 8 A.M. Ranger-led tours at 9 A.M. and 1 P.M., $1 fee.
Be mindful of the tides, which can cause extremely skinny water.

You needn't know all of this history to enjoy a kayak trip to Indian Key. The setting here is magnificent, with its background of oceanic blue water and its compact green island ringed on its western shore by a little beach. It's easy to find a launch site at the tiny park off U.S. 1 at MM 77.8. You can also rent kayaks from Florida Keys Kayak & Sail at MM 77.5 behind the Hungry Tarpon Restaurant.

wreckers venturing up from Key West flying the American flag and carrying official licenses to salvage goods from sunken ships. Key West soon became one of the most prosperous communities in America.

None of this was lost on John Housman, the son of a wealthy New Yorker. He decided to set up a wrecking center on Indian Key to challenge the hegemony of Key West's wreckers. He bought the key in 1831 and built a hotel, store, warehouse, homes, and cisterns to serve forty or fifty full-time inhabitants and many more transients intent on salvaging treasure from the treacherous offshore reef. In 1836 he even persuaded Florida's political establishment to declare Indian Key the county seat of brand-new Dade County—a ludicrous thought today!

But while fortunes were being plucked from the reef, American settlers on the mainland of Florida were pushing deeper into the Seminole Indians' dwindling territory. Three Seminole Wars broke out in the 1800s—the deadliest and most expensive Indian conflicts in U.S. history. In 1838, Dr. Henry Perrine began cultivating a tropical cornucopia, to include agaves, bananas, mangoes, coffee, tea, and other useful plants, on Indian Key. Two years later a hundred Seminoles attacked the key, killing several people including Dr. Perrine, who successfully hid his family in a turtle kraal beneath their house. The island was reduced to rubble. Today only a few vestiges of the buildings remain along the paths now cleared and labeled with their original street names. Perrine's agaves flourish, however, adding to this key's uniqueness.

Push off into the Atlantic Ocean and head directly south toward Indian Key. The water here is quite shallow; it's also a transparent aqua, making for great views both above and below the water. Boat traffic in the Indian Key Channels can be daunting, so keep to the skinny water. Under calm conditions it will take less than half an hour to reach the key; if you're battling an incoming tide off the ocean it will take a little longer. Head for the western shore of the key, where you'll find a small sandy beach and a high boat dock. (The eastern shore has sharp coral rocks which could damage your hull.)

Rangers lead informative tours at 9 A.M. and 1 P.M., but you can also ramble at will along the deserted streets of this diminutive town. Bring a book and a picnic lunch to enjoy under the rustling acacia trees. Climb up to the observatory platform towering high above Fourth Street. It offers a splendid view of the ruins amid a sea of agaves. As you look southward over the ocean you'll see the 135-foot tower marking Alligator Reef. A mile and a quarter off to the west lies the spot where the *San Pedro* met a watery grave in the hurricane of 1733. Today it is a state underwater archaeological preserve which you can explore by kayak. That trip's description begins below.

FYI:

Additional information on Indian Key can be obtained from

Indian Key Historic State Park
P.O. Box 1052
Islamorada, FL 33036
(305) 664-2540
www.dep.state.fl.us/parks

Trip # 10

The Wreck of the *San Pedro*

Launch Site: MM 77.8 (oceanside)
Location: Underwater archaeological preserve in 18 feet of water, 1¼ nautical miles south of Indian Key (24° 51.802' N, 80° 40.795' W)
Paddling Time: 1½ hours round-trip from launch site on U.S. 1
Comments: Wreck site of a 1733 Spanish treasure ship which can be explored by snorkeling or diving.
Note: Kayak rentals available at MM 77.5. You will need a compass to find the wreck site. Consult a tide table before planning your trip. Watch for strong tidal currents here. Bring at least one dive or snorkeling partner with you. A group of three or more is best. You will tie up to a mooring

buoy in eighteen feet of water. Practice getting out of your kayak and back into it in deep water before you take this trip. Do not take this trip if small-craft warnings are posted or if you are not confident of your paddling, swimming, snorkeling, or diving ability or of your ability to pull yourself into your kayak from deep water.

Here's a chance to get on the water and then into it! You can take this as a side trip from Indian Key or launch from the roadside park at MM 77.8 (oceanside), skirting the western shore of Indian Key before heading due south. With all of humanity behind you, you'll feel like an explorer as you paddle your small boat into the ocean, leaving Indian Key behind. On your right you'll see the southern shore of Lower Matecumbe Key; far back over your left shoulder will loom the tall steel tower marking Alligator Reef.

Within less than half an hour of passing Indian Key three white floating mooring balls will appear almost directly seaward from the long beach of Lower Matecumbe. Moor up here. Secure your paddle with rope or tight bungee cords and stow all gear. For safety's sake, first take turns

---

A plaque commemorating the wreck of the *San Pedro* lies on a sandy patch of ocean floor beneath the center of the mooring buoys. Ballast stones cover an area thirty by ninety feet; they include red ladrillo bricks from the ship's galley. Replica timbers, anchors, and a cannon can also be seen here. Spanish divers salvaged most of the *San Pedro's* cargo. Divers in the 1960s brought more silver coins, ceramics, riggings, hardware, and cannons to the surface. What remains is now protected by the state of Florida and by the ten species of coral that have encrusted the timbers and ballast stones. You will not find a huge, intact hull, as you might at Disney World. What you will find is one of Florida's first artificial reefs—full of parrotfish, moray eels, angelfish, lobsters, groupers, barracudas, schooling snappers and grunts, and clouds of brightly colored tropical reef fish. That and a lot of history, of course.

with your dive partner, swimming or snorkeling one at a time so that someone is in a kayak if assistance is needed. Take turns getting back into your boat before hoisting a dive flag and heading out to explore the site. Keep an eye on the weather. If winds or waves pick up, head back to Indian Key or the launch site. You are in the Atlantic Ocean, after all, at the site of a famous shipwreck.

As you slip on your face mask, think back to July 1733. Four armed Spanish galleons and eighteen merchantmen have just left Havana Harbor laden with silver, gold, jewels, rare spices, and other treasure. One sailor, Don Alfonso de Herrera Barragán, described what happened next:

> . . . we discovered the land of the Keys of Florida. At 9:00 that night the wind began to rise out of the north. It continued to freshen to the point where we all knew a hurricane was imminent. We found ourselves close to the said Keys, with the wind and sea so strong we were unable to govern ourselves, and each new gust came upon us with renewed major force. On the 15th, signs were made [among the fleet vessels] to try to arrive back to Havana, but we were unable to do so, for the wind went around to the south without slacking its force or lessening the seas. By 10:30 that night we had all grounded in the said Keys at a distance of 28 leagues in length. This capitana [flagship] grounded on one called Cayo Largo, two and one-half leagues from shore. I make assurance to Your Lordship that it was fortunate that we grounded, for if the contrary had occurred we would all have drowned because the hold was full of water and we were unable to pump it out.

Hearing news of the shipwreck from sailors aboard *Nuestra Señora del Rosario*, the only ship to escape grounding, Spanish officials in Havana dispatched nine rescue vessels full of supplies, divers, soldiers, and salvage equipment. They found the survivors clustered in small groups spread out across the Keys, protecting themselves from the tropical sun under pieces of debris cast up by the storm. After rescuing the survivors, the Spaniards turned their attention to salvaging the cargo. Some ships were refloated and towed back to Havana; others were burned to their waterlines so that divers could offload them. As testament to their remarkable efforts—and to the obvious smuggling rampant among the treasure fleets—a final accounting of the salvaged goods tallied more gold and silver than listed on the original ships' manifests!

FYI:

Additional information on this and other protected shipwrecks can be obtained from

Florida Department of State
Division of Historical Resources
Bureau of Archaeological Research
R. A. Gray Building
Tallahassee, FL 32399-0250
(805) 487-2299
dhr.dos.state.fl.us/bar/uap/uwsanped.html

Trip # 11

Long Key Bight and Beach

Launch Site: MM 71 (bayside) on Fiesta Key
Location: Long Key Bight to Long Key Point
Paddling Time: 2 hours
Comments: Lovely paddle across a bay, then along a coral beach at the Atlantic Ocean's edge.
Note: Camping available at nearby Long Key State Park. Bring a kayaking partner to help launch your boats over sharp coral rocks at the shoreline.

To reach the launch site, drive to the western end of the Channel 5 Bridge at MM 71. There is a small parking lot on the Gulf side of U.S. 1. There is no boat ramp here, but you can launch from a site under the bridge. Next to this is a section of the old Overseas Highway, now used as a fishing pier. The shoreline here is very rocky with sharp coral "boulders." Be careful portaging and launching your boat.

Head south under the bridge. It will take you about a half hour to paddle across Long Key Bight to the southeast tip of Long Key. The bight's shallow water and seagrass bottom provide the perfect habitat for near-

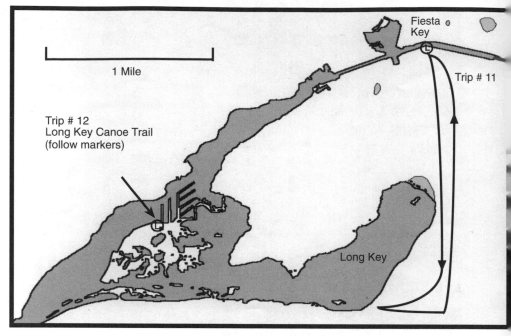

3.5. Long Key: Trips # 11–12

shore fishes, and you're likely to see flats fishermen resting on their poles here as they look for any sign of movement beneath the sea. Healthy deep green stands of tall mangroves line the shore ahead across the bight. Where the bight meets the ocean, the nearshore waters grow very shallow. Ahead of you is nothing but ocean. Behind you the new U.S. 1 bridge arches gracefully over the old Flagler bridge.

Turning west down Long Key's rattlesnake head, a coral beach begins to stretch out into the sea. Ocean currents carry flotsam and jetsam up to the shoreline, littering it with an impressive (and depressing) array of styrofoam and plastic. Still, there are no people here and no buildings or roads. The water here is perfect for swimming or snorkeling. (Watch out for upside-down jellyfish in some spots near shore. Wear water shoes or flippers to protect your feet.) Sea turtles nest on this wild beach, so respect their home. Offshore, you'll probably see a sailboat or two in Hawk Channel, and the low rise of the Long Key Aqueduct stretching west down the Keys. Other than that, the view is sky plus water plus beach.

Savor the view and the solitude. If weather conditions are right, you can paddle far down the western shore to the beach at Long Key State

Spanish sailors saw the Florida Keys for the first time just before Easter 1513. They named the archipelago Los Martires. To them these barrier islands looked like martyrs forlornly cast in the shallow seas. Their name for Long Key was Cayo Víbora—Rattlesnake Key.

Visitors since the Spanish have seen the Keys in a very different, softer light. Presidents, writers, and wealthy sport fishermen followed Henry Flagler's railroad down to Long Key at the turn of the twentieth century. Here they gathered at a prestigious gentlemen's fishing lodge extolling this beautiful, largely undeveloped island with its long ungroomed beaches, thick mangroves, and shallow-water bight filled with wading birds and thousands of tiny green baitfish.

Few kayakers frequent these waters. They should. In the winter when strong winds blow in from the north, Long Key Bight provides both shelter and beauty. Paddling farther around the southeastern end of the island and along the ocean's shore to Long Key Point keeps kayakers in the lee of the island's bulk, further blocking winter northerlies. The view out to sea here is amazing at any time of the year, especially at sunset.

Park. The shoreline suffered mightily here during Hurricane Georges in 1998, but new vegetation is taking hold thanks to an enormous restoration effort.

On the return leg of this trip you'll have a final look at coral and sand before heading back into the bight. Then you'll see a sliver of land and a huge swath of blue spanned by old and new U.S. 1. Tiny matchstick cars and trucks coast up and down the sleek new gray roadway, while below them the old span's columns reiterate their round arches like a Roman aqueduct. Nowhere else in the world does such a view exist.

FYI:

Campsites, for tents and RVs, can be reserved up to eleven months in advance by contacting

Long Key State Park
P.O. Box 776
Long Key, FL 33001
(800) 326-3521
www.dep.state.fl.us/parks

Trip # 12

Long Key State Park Canoe Trail

Launch Site: MM 67.5
Location: Long Key State Park, on an inland lagoon off Zane Grey Creek
Paddling Time: 1 to 1¼ hours
Comments: Pleasant easy paddle along an interpretive tidal-lagoon nature trail. Great for kids.
Note: Canoe rentals and camping available. Reservations recommended.

Park rangers on Long Key have nicknamed this lagoon the Cradle of the Ocean, and they've created a great little nature trail with signs and a brochure describing various features of this marine nursery and bird rookery. It's a nice place to get an introduction to Keys habitat and is very child-friendly. It's not as crowded as Pennekamp Park farther north and, because the lagoon is shallow and closed to motorboats, it's also quiet.

Calusa Indians lived on Long Key before Spanish sailors renamed it Cayo Víbora—for its rattlesnake shape, not its fauna—in the 1500s. Bahamian turtlers visited it too, but Long Key didn't take on any prominence until Henry Flagler's Overseas Railroad established a depot here in 1906. He also established the Long Key Fishing Club, which attracted talented saltwater anglers and America's rich and famous to its fancy lodge. Among them was writer Zane Grey, who popularized sailfishing and for whom a local waterway is named. Unlike most game fishermen (and famous writers) of his time, he preferred to catch and release his trophies—almost a century before it became fashionable (and ecologically sensible) to do so. The Long Key Fishing Club suffered the fate of most other buildings in the Upper Keys in 1935 when it fell victim to the Labor Day Hurricane. It was never rebuilt.

Hurricane Georges also hit Long Key hard in 1998. The park was closed for almost a year while downed trees and crushed structures were removed. Damage was particularly heavy on the park's nature-hike trail, where equipment and debris had to be carried in and out in a staggering number of garbage bags. The storm eroded much of the park's beach, but within months rangers had replanted it with sea purslane and sea oats. Today the park has a lighter tree canopy but is still rich in plant, bird, and marine life. The shallow offshore waters are excellent for snorkeling and sport fishing.

Not far from the park's entrance is a dock from which you can launch your kayak, or rent a canoe. Unlike the canoe trail at Pennekamp State Park, the trail here is fairly long, is very satisfying, and comes with a free brochure that guides you along a series of twenty stops. Each stop is marked by a clearly visible, numbered, white channel marker with a corresponding text in the naturalist brochure. You're urged to look for upside-down jellyfish (of which there are hundreds), marine worm casings, and soft corals. The lagoon is shallow but large, with plenty of passages into side lagoons or thick mangrove stands. You can stay on the route or wander about. And the far eastern end of the lagoon borders on Zane Grey Creek, which accesses the ocean.

Zane Grey is best known for his novels about cowboy life in the Old West, but he clearly loved his winter home in the Keys. In her excellent guidebook *The Florida Keys,* Joy Williams cites Zane Grey's farewell to a tarpon he hooked here: "Into my memory had been burned indelibly a picture of a sunlit, cloud-mirroring, green and gold bordered cove, above the center of which shone a glorious fish-creature in the air."

FYI:
Campsites, for tents and RVs, can be reserved up to eleven months in advance by calling (800) 326-3521. Additional information is available from

Long Key State Park
P.O. Box 776
Long Key, FL 33001
www.dep.state.fl.us/parks

Trip # 13

Curry Hammock State Park: A Paddle off Fat Deer Key

Launch Site: MM 56.1 (oceanside)
Location: Curry Hammock State Park, just north of Marathon
Paddling Time: 1 hour
Comments: Oceanside paddling along a nice beach in protected water. Exceptional fall hawk migration.

The Middle Keys constitute some of the most beautiful islands in the entire archipelago. They are slender strips of land spanned by long bridges. Here the expanse of the ocean meets the vastness of Florida Bay. Unfortunately, kayaking opportunities in the Middle Keys are limited because there is little public access to launch sites, currents in the broad channels here can be quite strong, and there are few nearshore "destinations" such as mangrove islands or patch reefs in this area. Powerboats predominate, speeding deepsea fishermen and snorkelers to the big reef out front.

There is only one real town here, Marathon, but houses, condos, and resorts cram the islands from tip to tip. Almost every speck of land is privately owned.

After an easy launch from the beach, a fifteen-minute paddle will take

---

At 260 acres, Curry Hammock State Park contains the largest uninhabited land parcel between Key Largo and Big Pine Key. The state began acquiring private property here in 1992, but it wasn't until seven years later that the park actually opened. There is no camping here, yet, but there is a beautiful beach with picnic tables and a bathhouse on the oceanside and a large upland hammock on both sides of U.S. 1.

A kiosk near the park entrance contains maps of the park. These show the broad outlines of Fat Deer Key, the peninsular Little Crawl Key, and tiny Deer Key just offshore.

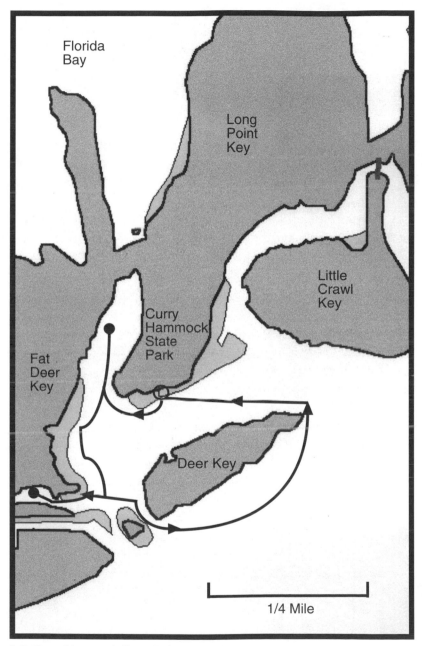

Florida
Bay

Long
Point
Key

Little
Crawl
Key

Curry
Hammock
State
Park

Fat
Deer
Key

Deer Key

1/4 Mile

3.6. Curry Hammock State Park: Trip # 13

you to the first of two shallow-water bays west of the picnic area. Small sharks cruise these bays, their fins slicing through the water like silver scythes. The mangroves here are full of birds, especially blue and white herons.

The park boundary lies just outside the westernmost bay. Here private boat channels and luxury homes cluster over what was, until the 1960s, a beautiful natural beach. Today it's Marathon Shores subdivision. Due east of this urban enclave lies Deer Key, a lovely park-owned island with a breathtaking view of the ocean. You can easily extend your trip by heading east out of the park's boundaries into the shallow waters off Grassy Key. On the way you will pass a resort called, appropriately, Valhalla.

Aside from leisurely kayaking, this area is also a good destination for snorkeling or fishing, and during the fall it is an excellent spot to observe the annual bird migration. The Florida Keys Raptor Migration Project sets up an observation site near the bathhouse. Peak migration occurs in mid-October.

FYI:

Additional information on Curry Hammock is available from

Long Key State Park

P.O. Box 776

Long Key, FL 33001

(305) 664-4815

www.dep.state.fl.us/parks

Information on the raptor migration is available from

Audubon of Florida

Tavernier Science Center

115 Indian Mound Trail

Tavernier, FL 33070

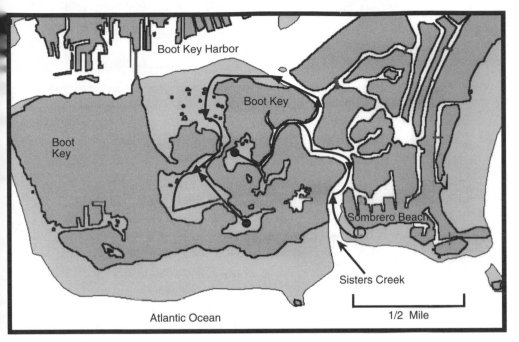

3.7. Sisters Creek, Marathon: Trip # 14

Trip # 14

Sisters Creek

Launch Site: MM 50.2 (oceanside) to Sombrero Beach Boulevard
Location: Mangrove Creek through Boot Key in Marathon
Paddling Time: 1½ hours
Comments: Paddle from a sandy oceanfront beach through a mangrove-lined creek with small lagoons.

To get to Sombrero Beach, turn onto Sombrero Beach Road at the stoplight near MM 50 in Marathon. You will pass a high school and many homes before seeing the park on your left. To launch your boat, park as far down the road as you can.

Driving through the city of Marathon can be a marathon in itself. There are so many strip malls catering to the needs of year-round residents and tourists that you rarely see the water or the natural vegetation that once covered Key Vaca. But Marathon has its charms— notably the beautiful Sombrero Beach. The burrowing owls that once thrived here took a hit during 1998's Hurricane Georges, but as if to say "I'm sorry," the hurricane also left a hefty amount of new sugary sand. The beach is a pleasant place to pass some time. It has picnic tables, a playground, rest rooms, even a shuffleboard court. At its far western end you can park your car and launch your kayak for a leisurely paddle through Sisters Creek.

From here the view out to sea is stunning. For this trip you'll head away from the ocean, turning right into the busy channel used by powerboaters speeding out to the reef and the Florida Straits. Stay on the right side of the channel and gape at the impressive homes there. You'll paddle for about fifteen minutes, with undeveloped Boot Key on your left. Then a "Slow—Minimum Wake" sign will signal a tributary opening up on your left. Cross the channel carefully (with an eye and ear attuned to the passage of fast boats) and enter this smaller creek. The noise will die down here, and the water become clearer. No prop turbidity here. After fifteen minutes this creek will open up into a large lagoon. It's a great place for bird-watching. Retracing your route out of the lagoon and back into the creek, you'll see a very small mangrove tunnel open up on your left. This is fun to explore, especially if your paddle separates in the middle so that you can use it as a canoe blade and to fend off low-lying mangrove branches. Here it'll be hard to believe you're in Marathon.

When you're done exploring this area, reenter the main creek as it curves north, then west. You'll see houses and a marina to your right in Boot Key Harbor and the 20th Avenue bridge ahead of you. Sailboats often anchor in this area. Bear left along the northeastern shore of Boot Key, watching for a small opening in the mangroves (by this point you'll have paddled for about twenty minutes since reentering the main channel). Take this opening to a thin creeklet which eventually opens up into a large lagoon full of egrets and songbirds. Red-winged blackbirds, warblers, and wrens fill the air with their songs, while dragonflies drone over the water. Upside-down jellyfish bob up from the floor of the lagoon.

Retracing your route, keep on the right side until you see Sombrero Beach. Then carefully cross the boat channel back to the launch site. There the beach awaits you. Swimming or shuffleboard, anyone?

Trip # 15

(Better than) Money Keys

Launch Site: MM 39.9 (bayside)
Location: Money Keys and Molasses Keys, just south of the Seven Mile Bridge
Paddling Time: 3 hours
Comments: Among the most beautiful islands anywhere.
Note: These islands lie just west of wide Moser Channel where oceanic waters rush into Florida Bay. Watch for strong tidal currents here. This trip is best taken near low tide so that you can explore the beautiful shallows and avoid deeper-draft boats. The trip between Money Key and the Molasses Keys is through unsheltered water; be confident of your paddling skills before taking it. Bring a friend along. Do not plan this trip for the first weekend in February—cars full of visitors to the Pigeon Key Arts Festival clog U.S. 1 in both directions—or on the second Saturday in April, when the bridge is closed for an annual marathon.

The launch site for this trip is at Veterans Park, a roadside pull-off on Little Duck Key at the western terminus of the Seven Mile Bridge. Known in its time as the eighth wonder of the world, it took Henry Flagler four years (1908–12) to build the original railway bridge. It had 546 piers with

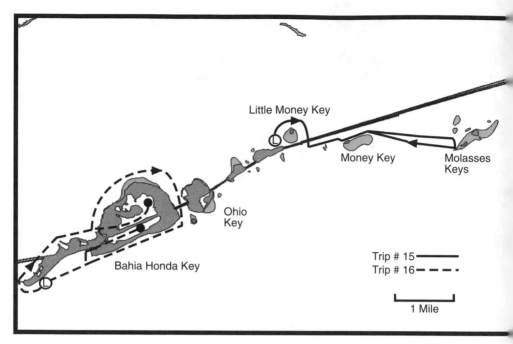

Little Money Key

Money Key

Molasses Keys

Ohio Key

Bahia Honda Key

Trip # 15 ——————
Trip # 16 — — — ·

1 Mile

3.8. Seven Mile Bridge and Bahia Honda: Trips # 15–16

underwater pilings made of a special German cement and secured to sea-floor bedrock. Four hundred men worked on the bridge's construction, living in a camp built on Pigeon Key. The story of their efforts is told in exhibits at the Pigeon Key Information Center on the eastern end of the bridge and at the Museums of Crane Point in Marathon.

You can also walk to Pigeon Key on a stretch of the old bridge. From the parking lot at the eastern end of the bridge you'll pass fishermen dangling their lines over the handrails into the water. Ospreys rest just under the top of the old roadbed. They're fascinating to watch. Keep an eye on the water too, especially on the bayside. About two-thirds of the way to Pigeon Key is a shallow flats frequented by huge spotted eagle rays. I've seen up to two dozen of these amazingly beautiful sea creatures here curling their white wing tips while they race just under the water's surface. If you're lucky, they might well leap into the air. Once you arrive at Pigeon

Key you can pay $8 and visit the homes that are being restored here by the Pigeon Key Foundation.

Amazingly, the original Seven Mile Bridge survived the 1935 Hurricane even though the Overseas Railroad tracks and locomotives didn't. In 1936 the Seven Mile underwent new construction to turn it into a highway for cars. For years motorists enjoyed unparalleled views, high above its graceful arches. Then in 1981 a Florida Keys Aqueduct Authority truck hit the propane tank underneath the bridge tender's house, sparking an explosion that closed the bridge for several days and halted ship traffic through Moser Channel for a year. A new Seven Mile Bridge opened in 1982. While it still provides lovely views and is high enough not to need a drawbridge, its architecture can't compete with that of the old span. Filmmakers immortalized a stretch of the old bridge in the mid-1990s when they used it to shoot the chase sequence in Arnold Schwarzenegger's movie *True Lies*.

Launch your kayak from the bayside boat ramp at Veterans Park and paddle just northeast of the launch to Little Money Key. There's a small defunct dock on its eastern shore and pleasant snorkeling in its shallow water. The views out to the Johnson Keys in Florida Bay are wonderful. From here, work your way south through the graceful gray arches of the old Seven Mile Bridge and under the considerably louder new span.

Money Key lies straight ahead, looking every bit like Gilligan's Island with its white sand beach and swaying coconut palms. Pull your kayak onto the sandy western shore and enjoy a rest from the twenty-minute paddle you've just taken. As you beachcomb you'll see cars zooming along the Seven Mile, but you probably won't hear them, especially from the island's south shore. Not only do coconut palms grow here but also a tiny bougainvillea and a poinciana, or flame tree, whose leaves were blown completely away by Hurricane Georges. If you're here near low tide, you'll probably have the island to yourself—there's a sandy shoal offshore that deters most boaters.

If you're confident of your paddling skills, push off from shore and work your way east through the skinny water just off Money Key. You're likely to paddle over sleeping nurse sharks, but keep an eye out for porpoises, tarpon, snook, and especially rays. The water will get deeper (about seventeen feet) after you've paddled for fifteen minutes or so, with far deeper water just to your right. It's another half hour of paddling, sometimes through rolling swells, to reach the Molasses Keys, so be sure that the tides and winds favor your trip.

You may find powerboats and sailboats anchored on the western side of the Molasses Keys. This area is just too pretty to resist. The larger island has a nice little sand beach, much used but not abused. Lobster traps that have floated ashore have been overturned as makeshift tables, and there is that rarest of Keys beach amenities, shade. Parts of the island are jagged coral, so wear shoes of some sort when exploring them. You'll find plenty of castaway shells alive with hermit crabs scurrying among tiny pieces of coral. Once I found an old aguardiente bottle with a Cuban label here. Who knows what you'll find.

It's about two miles back to the boat launch, so be sure to give yourself plenty of time. Stop for a break at Money Key, especially if it's sunset.

Trip # 16

Circumnavigating Bahia Honda Key

Launch Site: MM 38.9 (oceanside)
Location: Bahia Honda State Park
Paddling Time: 2 hours to circumnavigate the key, 1 hour more to explore interior lagoons
Comments: Bay and oceanside paddling around one of Florida's premier state parks with two interior lagoons.
Notes: Kayak rentals, camping, and three cabins are available. Reservations recommended. Watch out for strong tidal currents in Bahia Honda Channel.

The launch site is on the oceanside, opposite the visitor center. You'll see the kayak rental stand at the top of a set of wooden stairs that lead down to the beach. Portage your boat down the stairs and, depending on pre-

Bahia Honda is Spanish for "deep bay," and this is the deepest natural harbor in all the Florida Keys. It is also among the most beautiful, not only for its million-shaded blue water but for the high arches of yet another of Henry Flagler's magnificent bridges. A small portion of the bridge can be reached by a park trail, and it's well worth the walk, especially at sunset. The vistas high above the key are superlative.

You can also paddle underneath the bridge and then around the island, enjoying views into Florida Bay and out to sea. Beaches extend along the entire southern shore. Sandspur Beach, on the southeast corner of the key, has been named Best Beach in America. The nearshore waters are shallow, making for great snorkeling and swimming. The park has campsites, bathhouses, a snack bar, and a concession stand that rents kayaks and conducts snorkeling trips to nearby Looe Key Reef.

vailing winds, tide, and your own inclinations, push off to circle the key clockwise or counterclockwise. If you decide on the former, head down Logger Head Beach to your right. A short distance out in the ocean off the southwestern tip of the island is a tiny key. Although much prettier before Hurricane Georges raked it clean, this is a nice destination for novice paddlers, children, and anyone else who appreciates a great view. Whether you visit here or not, you'll want to round the western tip of Bahia Honda and head under the old Overseas Railroad bridge. Keep to the far right of the channel, mindful of boaters zipping out to the reef.

Paddling northeast, you'll pass the park's marina and then go under U.S. 1. Ahead on your right in a small inlet are the park's three rental cabins (a good deal, especially if there are several people in your party). About forty-five minutes after launching you'll see a very narrow inlet on the north central shore of the island. This leads into a large mangrove-lined lagoon. It is well worth exploring despite the sound of traffic on U.S. 1. Pelicans, herons, egrets, and ibis roost here, and the shallow waters serve as a marine nursery.

Outside the lagoon you'll have a panoramic view of Florida Bay as you paddle along Bahia Honda's northern shore. Then, as you round the key and head down its eastern shore, a huge American flag will come into view. This flies above neighboring Ohio Key, the southern portion of which will become part of the National Key Deer Refuge. You'll enter skinny water just before passing between Bahia Honda and Ohio Keys. Once again you'll paddle under the old highway's arches, the ocean's deep blue on the far horizon. Tall palms sway on Bahia Honda's eastern shore, and a tiny mangrove island just offshore offers a welcome pull-out spot. Here you can turn and watch carloads of people not as lucky as you are right now on your little island with an unobstructed view of ocean.

Bahia Honda's Atlantic shore fared poorly in Hurricane Georges. Sandspur Beach was closed for eight months between 1998 and 1999 as rangers rebuilt boardwalks, pavilions, rest rooms, campsites, and even the road there. Trees took a beating too, considerably thinning the once dense canopy. Nine thousand dollars' worth of new vegetation was planted in the hurricane's aftermath, and today the island's scars are slowly healing. Be sure to walk along the nature trail at the far eastern edge of Sandspur Beach's parking lot. It threads through one of the world's largest remaining stands of the threatened silver palm.

Just past the Sandspur Camping Area you'll see the bridge where the park's road passes over an inlet to a second interior lagoon. This tranquil area, which can be seen partially on the north side of the Sandspur parking area, is well worth exploring by kayak, especially in the winter months.

FYI:

Eighty campsites and three duplex cabins can be reserved up to eleven months in advance by calling (305) 872-2353. Boat rentals, snorkeling and parasailing can also be arranged in advance.

Additional information is available from

Bahia Honda State Park
36850 Overseas Highway
Big Pine Key, FL 33043
www.dep.state.fl.us/parks

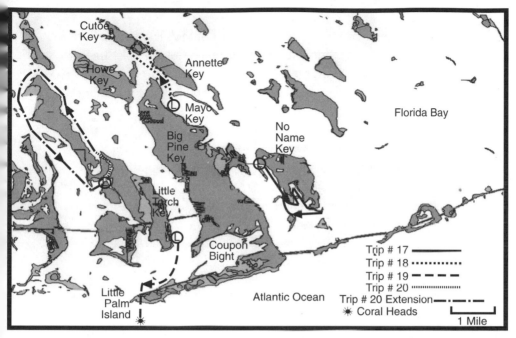

3.9. Big Pine Key Area: Trips # 17–20

Trip # 17

No Name Key: Around the Key Deer's Forest

Launch Site: MM 30.5 (bayside) on Big Pine Key to Wilder Road, then over the bridge to No Name Key
Location: No Name Key
Paddling Time: 2½ hours, 2 hours more to circumnavigate the key
Comments: Chance to see Key deer, explore two backcountry lagoons, and admire Bahia Honda Bridge.
Note: Reduced speed limits of 45 mph during the day and 35 mph at night on U.S. 1 are strictly enforced to protect the deer, which often graze along the roadside.

Less than half a mile from the turnoff for this trip's launch site is the Key Deer Bar & Grill, but make no mistake, it's not Key deer they're cooking. These diminutive deer, about the size of a cat as fawns, are protected by the Endangered Species Act, guarded by the National Key Deer Refuge, and much photographed by tourists.

Back in the 1940s settlers and visiting hunters had reduced the deer population to a total of fifty animals. But Jack Watson, a former hunter and the son of a Big Pine homesteader, took up the deer's cause, enlisting the help of journalists and members of Congress. The deer's toylike appearance—only two and a half feet high—intrigued cartoonist J. N. "Ding" Darling, whose nationally syndicated drawings introduced the public to these small cousins of Virginia white-tailed deer. Watson urged the creation of a refuge to protect the deer from poachers and land developers. The public and Congress responded. In 1957 the National Key Deer Refuge was created, making it illegal to harm the deer or their environment.

Most deer spotted along the road today sport radio-control tracking devices around their necks, giving them a somewhat robotic look. But just off the road, in the recesses of their pine rockland forest, are many more deer—as many as eight hundred, researchers say—roaming collarless through the scrub pine and saw palmetto.

You will probably see several deer when you cross over the bridge past the No Name Pub and Old Wooden Bridge Fish Camp at the end of Wilder Road. Having crossed Bogie Channel, you're now on No Name Key, an important settlement during the late 1800s, when No Name was one of the few Lower Keys islands with freshwater wetlands and aquifers. In 1870 forty-five people lived on the island, more than live there today. Additional homesteaders arrived on the Overseas Railroad, which reached No Name in 1912. By living on a parcel for at least five months of the year over a three-year period and making "improvements" to it (including clearing scarce forest or destroying the mangroves), settlers could receive legal deeds to the land. They did so despite relentless torment from mosquitoes once so thick that they blackened the white clapboard siding of island homes. A fierce hurricane in 1919, however, drove many pioneers back up the Keys to the mainland.

In 1928 a bridge linking No Name to neighboring Big Pine Key was completed, making it possible for people to drive up from Key West to No Name and then take a ferry from No Name to Marathon, where the road up the Keys resumed. Ten years later the old railroad tracks and bridges were converted into the Overseas Highway. The No Name ferry ceased to operate, and both residences and commercial activities moved to Big Pine Key, straddling U.S. 1. Today No Name Key hosts large tracts of federally protected Key deer habitat and residents bitterly split over whether the island should remain off the electric power grid. Many people built homes on the island precisely because they wanted to derive their energy from solar and wind-generated power. Others say real estate agents implied (or outright promised) that the island would soon plug into Big Pine's electric station, allowing them exactly the same comfortable modern lifestyle they enjoyed elsewhere. Today the latter circulate petitions for electrification while they power their homes with loud outside generators. Their neighbors circulate their own petitions, hoping to outlaw noise pollution and keep the island off the power grid. However this battle ends, one thing is certain—a paddle around the southern shore of No Name is a great way to unplug from the stresses of life in the new millenium.

To reach the launch site, turn bayside off U.S. 1 at the stoplight on Big Pine Key at MM 30.5. Bear right up Wilder Road, then turn left at the stop sign on South Street, and right at Avenue B. Follow Avenue B onto Watson Avenue. (There are signs for No Name Key along this route.) Within a few minutes you'll pass the No Name Pub and cross over the Bogie Channel bridge joining Big Pine and No Name Key. Pull onto the right shoulder of the road at the end of the bridge. There are two little launch sites here, both shaded by mangroves. Push off, working along the shoreline to your left. There are several small entrances to still lagoons here and an old pier. Small bonnethead and mud sharks frequent these waters, so be sure to look in the water while you paddle. Within a half hour of launching, a small lagoon will open up on your left. The calm, shallow water here acts like a magnifying glass illuminated by the tropical sun. If you look closely, you're likely to see many species of fish, even the hard-to-spot bonefish whose ghostlike appearance makes him the coveted prey of flats fly fishermen. Let your kayak drift with the current and you're likely to see each scale of a passing fish glisten clearly. This is your chance to exchange glances with a two-foot-long permit.

Herons, songbirds, and doves live here too, filling the air with their loud croaks, sweet melodies, and soft coos. And there are few better places to lean back in your boat and watch superwhite cumulus clouds mass and change shapes in a deep blue sky.

Exiting this lagoon, continue down the western shore of the island until you round a point of land and enter a much larger lagoon. Here on a summer day the sky can become your whole world. Huge, fat white cumulus clouds predominate. Water vapor seems to blossom in them, expanding their billowing mass like the popcorn kernels in an old-fashioned popper. Flat-bottomed thunderheads may race into view. These cumulonimbus clouds can tower more than twenty thousand feet in the air, infinite collages of deep gray and blue at their base with distinctive pure white anvil-shaped tops full of ice crystals. And you're likely to see something else high, high, high in the sky over your shoulder, looking like a white zeppelin-shaped toy balloon. Although it seems less than a quarter inch long, it's Fat Albert, the surveillance device taking snapshots of license plates in Havana.

Paddle or drift to the end of the lagoon, then make your way back up it. Working along the shoreline, you'll enter another, smaller lagoon opposite Big Mangrove Key. The southern tip of No Name Key lies just beyond this. From here you'll have an incredible view of both the old and new bridges spanning the wide Bahia Honda Channel. On a clear day you'll be able to make out individual sailboats moored in the state park's marina, but this will be the only speck of human habitation that you'll see. Enjoy the view. The graceful arches of the old Overseas Highway bridge are a steel echo of the days of Henry Flagler and his railroad, and it's nice to imagine a heron's view of a railcar's silhouette crossing the gingerbread bridge. The new U.S. 1 bridge, closer to Big Pine Key, seems more Art Deco in shape. Its light gray concrete arches are much lower as they span the water, their perfect semicircles forming a pleasant pattern against the channel's intense blue. They give off a more confident, modern air—the feel of an automobile, not a turn-of-the-century railcar.

5. Key deer, with and without radio collar

You can continue paddling up No Name's eastern shore from here (it will add about two hours to your trip). From there you'll see Little Pine and the Johnson Keys, marking the edge of the Key deer's habitat. If you retrace your route past the lagoons you've visited, hugging the key's western shore, your view will include the bridge linking Big Pine to No Name. It's low, straight, and utilitarian—a bridge meant to get from one point to another without magic or fanfare. A bridge where fishermen can cast a line, where neighborhood kids ride bikes at sunset, and tourists drive with their windows rolled down, cameras at the ready. A bridge that often hears tiny hoofbeats as diminutive deer venture out of their forest home.

FYI:

For additional information about the Key deer, their habitat, and how to protect them, contact

Florida Keys National Wildlife Refuges
P.O. Box 430510
Big Pine Key, FL 33043-0510
(305) 872-0774

You can also get firsthand information on the deer and their environment, and on hiking trails in Big Pine's pine rockland forest, hardwood hammock, and mangrove forest, by stopping at the National Key Deer Refuge visitor center in the Big Pine Key Plaza off Key Deer Boulevard, an eighth of a mile mile north of the traffic light on U.S. 1. It's open Monday to Friday, 8 A.M. to 5 P.M.

Trip # 18

Exploring the Tidal Creeks of Cutoe Key

Launch Site: MM 30.5 (bayside) on Big Pine Key to the end of Key Deer Boulevard
Location: Backcountry tidal creeks south of Cutoe Key
Paddling Time: 2½ hours, 1 hour more to circumnavigate the key
Comments: Paddling across two backcountry channels and among tidal creeks.
Note: If a strong northern wind is blowing, you might want to postpone this trip and choose a destination that's more protected from the wind.

To reach the launch site, turn bayside at the stoplight near MM 30.5 on U.S. 1. Drive up Key Deer Boulevard past Big Pine's shopping center, baseball fields, and miles of pine scrublands until you reach the Blue Hole. Turn right onto Big Pine Street, then take the second left onto Koehn Boulevard. At the end of this street is a little-used boat ramp. You'll see Mayo Key ahead of you across the channel on your right and much bigger Annette Key on its left. After launching, head across the channel for

From Big Pine Key you can launch and paddle through a very different backcountry habitat within the boundaries of yet another wildlife refuge, the Great White Heron National Wildlife Refuge. Covering 264 square miles of water at the southeastern corner of the Gulf of Mexico, this refuge was among the first established in Florida. Its namesake, the great white heron, is a color variant of the great blue heron and is the largest wading bird in North America. Plume hunters nearly exterminated this species, but today the protection offered it is shared by other rare birds such as the West Indian white-crowned pigeon, the roseate spoonbill, and the only colony of laughing gulls in the Lower Keys. Because the waters of this wildlife refuge are so shallow, they are a paradise for kayakers. The only other boaters you will likely see up close are flats fishermen, often poling their boats. Powerboaters must stick to the deeper channels.

Annette Key's southern shore. You'll pass an area marked on nautical charts as The Grasses, named for the seagrass beds that lie here. Annette is a fairly long key unbroken by bays, creeks, or inlets. Continue northwest along its mangrove-lined shore for about an hour until you reach the channel that separates Annette from Cutoe Key.

As you approach Cutoe, the outlines of a tidal creek on the right side of the island will become clear. Head for it. As you paddle you'll see Big and Little Spanish Keys off to the east. Beyond them is nothing but the turquoise water of the Gulf. Entering the creek's sheltered waters, you'll find peace and warmth—and birds, lots of birds. Here flocks of ibis fill the air, as do the various members of the egret family—great egrets standing on snags and branches poking out of the water, snowy egrets with lacy crests perched in the trees, reddish egrets with dark gray bodies and rust-colored heads. Joining the refuge's namesake great white heron are little blue herons (which are white as juveniles) and yellow-crested night herons, among the most strikingly beautiful birds in breeding season when they sport two-inch long white plumes from their bright yellow crowns. If your neck gets cramped looking up at this wealth of birdlife, look down into the water as well. You may see a dark shadow explode under your boat—probably a southern stingray. Sharks love these tidal passages, too. They're fascinating to watch and can usually provide a little spurt of adrenaline, even when you're observing them from safely aboard your kayak.

Exploring the tidal creeks here is a pleasant way to spend a morning or afternoon, but be sure to identify landmarks along the way or tie a piece of bright-colored tape or cloth to a low-lying mangrove so that you can find your way back to the channel that separates Cutoe from Annette Key. All of the masses of green mangrove-covered islands can begin to look alike. Also, the southeastern shore of Howe Key can obscure the northern tip of Big Pine Key from this vantage point.

Depending on the winds and tide, you can retrace your route back across the channel to Annette Key and down its shore or head in a diagonal line from the southwestern islet off Cutoe Key to the northern tip of Big Pine and down its shore to the boat launch.

FYI:

Additional information about the Great White Heron National Wildlife Refuge can be obtained from

Florida Keys National Wildlife Refuges
P.O. Box 43050
Big Pine Key, FL 33043-0510
(305) 872-0774

or visit the National Key Deer Refuge visitor center in the Big Pine Key Plaza off Key Deer Boulevard, an eighth of a mile north of the traffic light on U.S. 1. It's open Monday to Friday, 8 A.M. to 5 P.M.

Trip # 19

Snorkeling the Patch Reefs off the Newfound Harbor Keys

Launch Site: MM 28.3 (oceanside) onto Pirates Way, then Jolly Roger Drive on Little Torch Key

Location: Patch reefs off the Newfound Harbor Keys south of Big Pine Key

Paddling Time: 2½ hours round-trip to reef, 1 to 2 hours more to explore the Newfound Harbor Keys

Comments: Patch reef near shore with mooring buoys and a chain of oceanside Keys to explore.

Note: This trip is best taken in summer or fall when water clarity is best and crowds are thin.

Bring a dive flag and at least one dive or snorkeling partner with you. You will tie up to a mooring buoy in ten feet of water. Practice getting out of and back into your kayak in deep water before you take this trip. Do not take this trip if small craft warnings are posted or if you are not confident of your swimming or snorkeling ability or your ability to pull yourself into your kayak from deep water.

To reach the launch site, turn toward the ocean onto Pirates Way at MM 28.3 on Little Torch Key. A short drive will lead you to a sharp left turn just past the sign for the Nature Conservancy's Torchwood Nature Preserve. Continue down the dead-end street you're now on, Jolly Roger Drive, and unload your kayak at a small put-in site on the right side at the end of the road. This is a residential neighborhood with little street parking, so pull your car up the street a bit, making sure that you're not blocking anyone's driveway.

After pushing off, paddle down the south shore of Little Torch Key over the very skinny, translucent nearshore water. On your right you'll

---

This trip starts from a site owned by the Nature Conservancy, skirts the shore of exclusive Little Palm Island, and ends up underwater in a nearshore coral reef. Mooring buoys above the reef let you tie your kayak up safely, but if you're not confident of your deepwater abilities or don't feel like swimming or snorkeling (or if you have children with you), this still is a pretty trip to take. When you reach the ocean, you can explore the passages between the Newfound Harbor Keys instead of snorkeling.

have a nice view of the Torchwood Preserve, unmarred by development. Powerboats will zoom past you on your left, heading out to the blue water through busy Newfound Channel. Clear nose skates, rays, and sharks are common sights in this area, where the shallow, limpid water acts like a bell jar, magnifying every feature.

After about ten minutes of paddling, Little Torch will begin curving to your right. Here you should head across Newfound Harbor Channel instead, setting your sights on the pinkish rooftops of Little Palm Island, the farthest right (west) small key of the group of islands on the left side of the channel. (Little Palm Island is not named on nautical charts; it's only shown as a small key just west of the largest Newfound Harbor Key.) It will take about twenty minutes to complete the crossing to three tiny mangrove islets. Any of these little specks of land makes a good rest spot to reapply sunscreen, sip on a water bottle, and enjoy the view. The Newfound Harbor Keys and Little Palm Island are privately owned, so this is the last terra firma you'll visit until you're back on Little Torch Key.

The first island is round and covered completely with mangroves. You can pull up here and catch your breath. There is a little sand beach on the second of the islands (on my last trip someone had set a barbecue grill in the middle of it). The third little islet is often covered with birds of all types—herons, ibis, egrets, pelicans, and magnificent frigate birds. They'll squawk and clack mightily as you paddle past them into a beautiful underwater sponge garden. Here you'll find huge loggerhead sponges, graceful vase sponges, and painful orange fire sponges (don't touch!). If you're lucky, you'll also see a rare and lovely Bahama star. These incredible starfish are an elegant red-orange, a spectacular sight set against the white sand bottom in these waters. Also known as cushion stars, they are the largest sea stars in Florida, reaching up to twenty inches in size. Harvested to the brink of extinction, Bahama stars are now on the endangered species list, with strict financial penalties for those who pluck them from the sea.

The four-star accommodations of Little Palm Island are beautiful too—teak furniture strewn across the grounds, chic canvas umbrellas at the ready, palm-thatched roofs and tiki bars straight out of Shangri-La. If you prefer sea stars and other beauties that lie beneath the sea (or if you haven't called ahead for reservations), keep paddling past Little Palm through the deeper water that lies at the mouth of Newfound Harbor Channel. After heading out into the Atlantic Ocean, curve to your left. You'll soon see the first orange mooring buoy a few hundred yards out to sea. Several white buoys are anchored just beyond this one, off the white sand beach of Big Munson Island. Carefully tie up your boat, hoist your dive flag, and take turns with your snorkeling partner exploring the water. Once you've both successfully gotten out of and back into your kayaks, it's dive time.

The coral heads here are not as healthy as elsewhere in the Keys, perhaps because of the turbidity and pollution caused by human habitation and powerboating. Still, parrotfish, pork fish, wrasses, and grunts abound, and you can have great fun herding tropical fish in and around the coral heads. There watchful barracudas patrol the perimeter. Don't let the barracudas' stealth and large teeth scare you, but do leave your shiny jewelry or watch in your boat—barracudas think they're fish and will come in for a closer look.

If you've decided not to snorkel, you can soak up the ocean views by paddling east up the Newfound Harbor Keys chain. The patch reef continues beneath the water, in a parallel line about a quarter mile (ten minutes' paddle) offshore. If the sea is calm, you'll probably see brain coral beneath your boat. Over your left shoulder is another very tropical view—beautiful sand beaches and weathered houses (private residences) on Big Munson and Cook's Island. If this reminds you of the South Seas, you might want to head to a video store when you get back on land and rent the movie *PT 109*. That film about John F. Kennedy's navy days was filmed on Little Palm Island.

You can pass from the ocean into more sheltered waters on the north side of any of these islands, except at low tide, when you'll find skinny water and a very mucky bottom on either side of the island chain. A power line runs overhead just off the north side of these Keys, somewhat detracting from the view. Still, the waters here teem with life, as do the trees. Here Coupon Bight opens as it flows to the ocean. It's a rich and varied nursery well worth exploring before you head back across Newfound Harbor Channel to Little Torch Key.

After you've enjoyed your time in the water, you'll eventually hoist yourself back into your kayak for a paddle around Little Palm and through the Channel and the skinny water to Little Torch Key. If you've planned well, you'll have a cooler full of chilled mango and pineapple slices waiting for you in the trunk of your car.

FYI:

Additional information about the Torchwood Nature Preserve can be obtained from

The Nature Conservancy
Florida Keys Office
P.O. Box 4958
Key West, FL 33041
(305) 296-3880

Trip # 20

Getting Lost in the Torches

Launch Site: MM 27.9 (bayside) onto Middle Torch Road
Location: Middle and Big Torch Keys
Paddling Time: 1 to 5 hours
Comments: One-hour paddle through two beautiful shallow lagoons protected from strong winds. Suitable for kids. This trip can be expanded into a five-hour circumnavigation of Big Torch Key.

To get to the launch site, turn bayside off U.S. 1 at MM 27.9. This will put you on Middle Torch Road. Follow it for two and a half miles until you see a sign on your left for Big Torch Key. Take this turn and continue for about half a mile until the road becomes a low causeway with water on both sides. Park here on the right shoulder and launch your kayak into the small lagoon immediately in front of you. Head out, keeping to the left of the little island in the middle. Keep paddling straight ahead toward the lone house at the end of the lagoon. Then, just before reaching the house, you'll see an opening in the mangroves to your left. Here you'll pass through a narrow, extremely shallow cut, about a kayak's width

The extremely shallow waters around Little, Middle, and Big Torch Keys afford some of the prettiest green kayaking in the Keys. Most of the water immediately surrounding these islands is one foot or less deep at low mean tide, which means that in places it feels more like sculling than kayaking. Nevertheless, the remoteness and tranquil beauty here are reason enough to pull off U.S. 1 just before Torch-Ramrod Channel. Bird life thrives in these islands, making sunrise a peak choice for launching. The only downside to kayaking here is that the low profile of these tightly packed mangrove islands can make navigation confusing if not completely confounding. Study a chart before launching, and be particularly observant of your surroundings.

across. This opens up into a much larger body of water with another tiny mangrove island ahead of you, just off the northwestern tip of Middle Torch Key. By going around the left (west) side of this island, you'll see the opening to another beautiful lagoon. It will take about half an hour to paddle its entire shoreline.

If you'd like to expand this one-hour trip, you can retrace your route out of this second lagoon, then head north along the eastern shoreline of Big Torch Key. It will take you about two hours to reach the northern tip of this sprawling island. It's a remote area with very shallow water, so your only companions will likely be wading birds, rays, sharks, and other backcountry residents. From the northern tip of Big Torch you'll be able to see the Content Keys (described in trip # 21). The northwestern shore of Big Torch is among the prettiest places in the Lower Keys, translucent water peppered with mangrove trees alive with hundreds of ibis, herons, and egrets. Healthy seagrass beds pulsate with juvenile fish and fast-moving rays. Sponges dot the seafloor.

Two hours of paddling will bring you down Big Torch's western shoreline, still largely uninhabited. Hold close to the shoreline as it curls east back toward the causeway where you parked. Otherwise it's easy to get lost amid all the green.

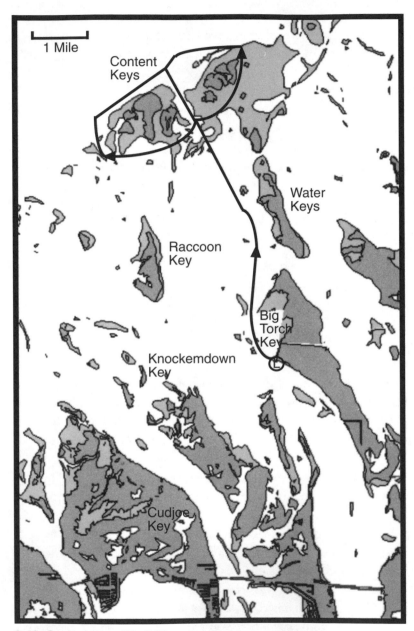

3.10. Content Keys: Trip # 21

Trip # 21

Out to the Content Keys

Launch Site: MM 27.9 (bayside) onto Middle Torch Road to Big Torch Key

Location: Content Keys in the Gulf of Mexico, 3 miles north of Big Torch Key

Paddling Time: 6 1/2 hours (this is the longest trip described in this book)

Comments: A long paddle across the backcountry to a beautiful island group ringed by shoals and separated by tidal creeks.

Note: This is a very rewarding trip to take if you're strong and confident in your paddling abilities. Bring along a kayaking partner, a compass, at least two gallons of water per person, an anchor, a rope, a hat, and plenty of sunscreen. Let someone know where you're going and when you expect to be back. There is little boat traffic in this isolated area, and it's a long swim back to shore. Examine the tide tables closely, and don't attempt this trip if you'll be battling an incoming tide or strong winds on either leg of your journey. It could double your paddling time. Be particularly cautious of the strong current that rushes in and out through Content Passage. It could easily sweep you into the deep water of the Gulf of Mexico. Finally, at extreme low tide, passage through some of the Contents and near the northern tip of Big Torch Key will be difficult.

If you like white shoals glistening in turquoise water, long vistas with no signs of human habitation, or exploring every twisted turn through tidal creeks, you'll be very content with this trip. The Content (accent on the first syllable) Keys lie at the northern boundary of the Great White Heron National Wildlife Refuge, about as far away from shore as you can safely get in a kayak.

Getting to the launch site is a bit of a journey in itself. Turn off U.S. 1 (bayside) onto Middle Torch Road and follow it for two and a half miles through low scrubland and a few houses here and there. The Torch Keys are named in honor of the torchwood tree, but few remain here after the efforts of homesteaders to clear the land for pineapple and key lime cultivation. You are likely to see flocks of ibis curving through the air and maybe a Key deer or two, but keep your eye out here for snakes, too. I once spotted a huge rattlesnake crossing this road. I sat in my car, staring out the window, as it coiled up less than ten feet from me. Watch too for the sign marking the turnoff to Big Torch Key, and turn left at it, following the road for another six miles until you come to a dead end. Before you unload your gear, walk down the little trail that heads off to the right of the steel barrier. You'll put your boat into the water here, so study the indentations in the coral rock in advance. It's easy to lose your footing here, especially portaging a boat.

Launch your boat, and as you emerge from the mangroves, consider tying a brightly colored piece of cloth to a branch to mark the launch site. Then head right (north) around the western point of Big Torch Key. Several small mangrove islets lie ahead on your left. Paddle between these and the shoreline of Big Torch. The water in this area is shallow and filled with a healthy hardbottom community of huge loggerhead sponges (some almost as big as a kayak), vase sponges, crabs, and lobsters. You'll also see healthy beds of turtle grass, unscarred by engine props. And where there's turtle grass, there are also turtles. I've seen several in this area, looking like brown logs drifting in the blue water. They'll often look right at you with their incredibly large black eyes before dipping their heads and paddling off. When it's sunny and the water is calm, this area is magical. The water becomes totally transparent, the sky is incredibly large, and you'll have a 720-degree view all to yourself—360 degrees of visibility above the surface, 360 degrees below it. As you paddle, you'll make ripples, and the play of sunlight on the undulating surface will be hypnotic.

Continue working your way north, paralleling the western shore of Big Torch. After about an hour you'll be between the first of the Water Keys, on your right, and Raccoon Key on your left. Resist the temptation to pull up on Raccoon Key. Raccoons do live in the Florida Keys, including a rare local variety with yellow fur, but until very recently rhesus monkeys lived here, held captive on the island by a stout steel fence (although a few were reported to have escaped during Hurricane Georges). They and a similar population of monkeys kept on Key Lois in the Atlantic Ocean were raised by an out-of-state company as lab animals. Both populations have repeatedly been ordered to be removed, with state lawyers, federal lawyers, and corporate lawyers all pleading their cases. The legal fur is apparently no longer flying, and the monkeys are gone, but unless you like tall fences and bad karma, give Raccoon Key a wide berth.

As you paddle for another hour along the Water Keys' western shore, take a look around for a geography lesson. Little Crane Key lies on your left, midway between Raccoon Key and the Western Contents. Out five miles past that, arching southwest toward Key West, are Riding Key and the half-moon island group of Sawyer Key. On a clear, still day you'll even see the Johnson Key mangroves and the tip of the Barracuda Keys. Views like this accentuate your visual alertness, but no one sense here need be ascendant. Although most people focus on the visual superlatives of the Florida Keys, a warm breeze against your face, the smell and taste of salt water, the beating of a bird's wings overhead, and the pleasant feeling of slipping your legs into the silky warm water—all these other sensations vie with the visual.

Almost three hours after leaving your car, you'll arrive at Content Passage. Now you'll choose whether to explore the Eastern or the Western Content Keys. (Unless you've started early, are paddling a cockpit-style ruddered kayak, or are a marathoner, you won't have time to explore both.) The eastern group will take less time to explore, because it is closer to the Water Keys and because the individual islands are smaller. A large shoal rings this group, and a tidal creek winds through it. To visit the western group you'll cross the fairly wide Content Passage. As you reach the western group, you'll encounter calm waters brimming with fish. A small lagoon shelters sharks and wading birds. Either group of islands is paradisical, especially when strong sunlight plays on the white sandbars. Your time here will be well spent, but it will also be dictated by the tide and wind. You'll have to retrace your route before sunset, so be sure to give yourself ample time.

Paddling back, you'll enjoy an extraordinary view as the curvature of

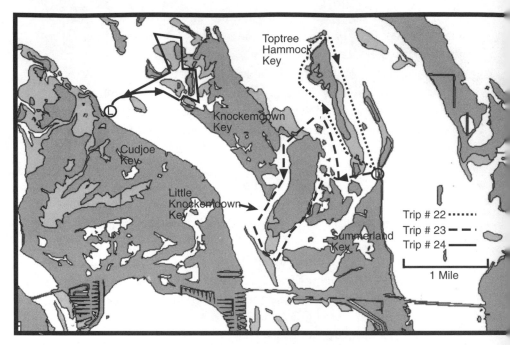

3.11. Toptree Hammock and Knockemdown Keys: Trips # 22–24

the earth makes things that are obviously real, like buildings and high-ways, disappear entirely, then reemerge floating in miniature on the rim of what looks like an infinitely delicate turquoise teacup. Two white squares lie on the far horizon. In a half hour they'll separate into two houses, one entirely white, one partially green. Thirty minutes later they'll cease floating and descend into a pale gray line. As you draw nearer, the line becomes a landmass, then a road, then coral rock adjacent to the road. The houses are two of those you drove past earlier today on the winding road between Middle and Big Torch Keys.

After a very long paddle you'll draw abreast of the house that sits on one of the bays of Big Torch Key. Look closely among the mangroves, and in fifteen minutes you'll spot the old empty milk jug hanging from a mangrove branch. It (and any cloth you might have tied to a branch ear-lier) signals the otherwise indiscernible cut through the mangrove bank into the tiny harbor of the launch site.

Trip # 22

Circumnavigating Toptree Hammock Key

Launch Site: MM 25 (bayside), onto Niles Road on Summerland Key
Location: Toptree Hammock Key, north of Summerland Key
Paddling Time: 1¾ to 2 hours
Comments: Easy paddle through shallow, protected backcountry waters and around an uninhabited island.
Note: The water here is skinny, between one and three feet, so check the tide table before heading out. Avoid paddling here at low tide or you may be a stick-in-the-mud.

To get to the launch site, turn off U.S. 1 at MM 25, heading down Horace Street next to Monte's Seafood Restaurant. Take the second right and then jog to the left onto Niles Road. It will end at a small boat ramp next to a large fence. Unload your gear and park up the road a bit, away from the gate.

You'll see a few mangrove islets ahead to your right. Head for these, working your way north across some very skinny water. You'll see Little Knockemdown Key over your left shoulder just west of here, with a few houses lining its shore. The dark green curve of Toptree Hammock is

When you're kayaking the Keys, sometimes the skinniest water is the most rewarding. Here you're sure to have the place to yourself because other boaters draw so much more water than you do. Aside from solitude, you'll reap other benefits, too. You'll be able to see sponges and sea cucumbers only a few inches away, for example, and you're bound to drift over sleeping sharks. The backcountry waters north of Summerland Key are a perfect place to idle away a few hours or a whole day, and Toptree Hammock is particularly nice.

ahead of you, north of Little Knockemdown, in a shoal extending from the mangrove islets.

It will take about forty-five minutes to paddle up the western shore to Toptree Hammock's northern tip. Along the way you'll see birds festooning the trees, chattering and croaking loudly as you pass. Beneath the water on this side of the key is a healthy hardbottom community full of loggerhead, vase, and column sponges and the odd-looking Florida sea cucumber, a ten-inch-long, woolly-looking, bumpy brown echinoderm that is (reportedly) edible. The view west to the uninhabited shoreline of Knockemdown Key may inspire you to explore it. It will take less than an hour to reach it, but the key's more interesting northwestern shore is easier to reach from Cudjoe Key.

As you round the northern tip of Toptree Hammock, you will see Raccoon Key, the Contents, and Big Torch Key sprawling into the Gulf of Mexico. Here the water is shallow enough to ward off powerboats, clear enough to hypnotize those who peer into it. The water is a shape-shifter—one moment it resembles liquid mercury rolling towards the horizon, the next it looks like hammered stainless steel or pewter. When schools of hundreds of tiny baitfish leap in front of your kayak, it's as if silver rain is falling upward.

On the paddle back down the eastern side of Toptree Hammock, two small once-inhabited islands will come into view. Then you'll see Leda's Bridge, which once linked these islands to Summerland Key. It's a pretty sight, and a good reminder of how crowded the Keys could have become if development had gone unchecked.

Trip # 23

Circumnavigating Little Knockemdown Key

Launch Site: MM 25 (bayside), onto Niles Road on Summerland Key
Location: Little Knockemdown Key, north of Summerland Key
Paddling Time: 2¼ hours

This trip leaves from the launch site used for the trip to Toptree Hammock Key. Both of these keys lie north of Summerland Key in shallow water that's protected from strong winds. In winter they're a good destination for bird-watchers, and they're particularly nice spots to watch the sun rise or set. Unlike uninhabited Toptree Hammock, Little Knockemdown has some houses, but they're nicely weathered stilt homes that seem at ease with the landscape.

Comments: Easy paddle around a backcountry key.

Note: Little Knockemdown Key is surrounded by a narrow channel that's deeper than the surrounding skinny water. While this is an advantage, it also has a swift current that can be hard to work against when the tide is coming in. Check the tide table before heading out.

To reach the launch site, turn north off U.S. 1 at MM 25 onto Horace Street and drive past Monte's Seafood Restaurant. Take the second right, then jog to the left onto Niles Road. At the end of the road is a boat ramp. Park away from the gate to a private residence. Once you've launched your kayak, head for the two mangrove islets you see ahead of you on your right.

From here head straight across the water separating Little Knockemdown from Summerland Key. Toptree Hammock Key is off to your right; you may see an aluminum shed on it. Far in the distance the Content Keys shimmer, poised on the edge of the Gulf of Mexico. A boat hull sits in the water just off the northern tip of Little Knockemdown. Veer to the left here, just past one of the stilt houses that dot the island. Most of the water in this area is very shallow, so work your way closer to the shore, where you'll find a nice channel (roadless Little Knockemdowners use it to bring in supplies). The channel here can be swift when you're riding a tide. Admire the view of bulky Knockemdown Key as it recedes behind you. Up ahead of you on the right is Cudjoe Key, Fat Albert the surveillance airship's home base.

As you round the southern tip of Little Knockemdown Key, you'll have a glimpse of the old Overseas Highway bridge with its elegant arches.

Then work your way back up the eastern shore of Little Knockemdown to the launch site on Summerland Key to your right.

It's a simple trip, but given the interplay of sun, wind, and water it will be different every time.

Trip # 24

The Bay on Knockemdown Key

Launch Site: MM 21.5 (bayside) to Blimp Road on Cudjoe Key
Location: Shallow-water bay with several mangrove islets on the northwest shore of Knockemdown Key
Paddling Time: 1 hour
Comments: A quick paddle to a good birding spot in a protected bay.
Note: Crossing Kemp Channel can be very difficult during strong winter blows from the north-northwest.

The launch site is on Cudjoe Key. To reach it, turn bayside off U. S. 1 at MM 21.5 onto Blimp Road. The blimp is Fat Albert, a navy surveillance airship. Its base is located off this road, visible but marked with No Trespassing signs. Although it's used primarily to keep tabs on developments in Cuba and monitor drug trafficking, the fact that Fat Albert floats above the Keys only in good weather makes it a handy tool for kayakers. If servicemen start pulling Fat Albert down, head for shore—rain and wind are on the way. Where else but in the Keys would kayakers have a giant tethered white blimp (virtually identical to the old Nickelodeon mascot minus the orange lettering) as their bellwether?

As you head down the road past Fat Albert's home base, murmur a word of thanks to all the Keys residents and their supporters who blocked a missile test site here. You may have seen bumper stickers championing this cause, which was settled for good only in 1999. Air force top brass wanted to shoot 26,000-pound missiles from lowly Cudjoe Key to targets off the Florida Panhandle. (An alternate base choice was lovely, pristine St. Joseph Peninsula State Park on Apalachicola Bay near Tallahassee.)

Knockemdown Key, like its neighbors Little Knockemdown and Toptree Hammock, is a great kayaking destination. While it's much bigger than these keys, a trip around it can be rewarding, offering pleasant backcountry scenery, shallow water and shoals, and abundant bird life. A circumnavigation of the key takes about three hours by kayak, providing the wind's not too strong.

A short trip to the bay on Knockemdown's northwestern shore can provide a time-challenged paddler with these same rewards in only an hour. This makes it a great trip at the beginning or end of a workday, a nice chance to loosen up if bad weather has kept you housebound, or an introductory trip for novice kayakers or older kids.

The Star Wars scenario then called for defense missiles at Eglin Air Force Base in the Panhandle to destroy the incoming missives from the Keys. The fact that three national wildlife refuges near Cudjoe Key were under federal protection didn't register on Washington's radar until a grassroots movement united local residents—some of whom had previously opposed the refuges. If the threats posed by pollutants weren't sufficient cause for concern, the notion of halting traffic along the only road linking one key to another and barring all boats from local waters for large periods before and after each test firing was. The plan is now dead, a mere footnote to the modern history of the Keys.

Blimp Road ends at a boat launch on Kemp Channel. Powerboats and sailboats use this ramp, so after unloading your gear, park far up from the ramp itself. As you look out east over the channel, you'll see a small mangrove island midway between Cudjoe Key and Knockemdown. Pelicans, cormorants, egrets, and herons crowd this island, squawking loudly enough to be heard on both shores. It's quicker to paddle past this key on the north (left) side, but if the wind is up, stay in the lee of the island and round its southern tip. After passing this island, head across the remainder of Kemp Channel. It will take you a little over fifteen minutes to make the crossing from the boat launch to the entrance of a large, protected bay dotted with several mangrove islets. The water here is warm and shallow year-round—so shallow at times that you'll have to scoot your boat forward or portage it over scattered shoals. Consider this a small cost for having your very own "instant beach" with beautiful vistas out over the backcountry through the Budd Keys. There is plenty of gentle exploring to do in these wildlife-rich waters, but because it's so peaceful here, I often take a book with me, tie up to a mangrove, and dangle my legs over the side of my boat. Sometimes I wave to Fat Albert.

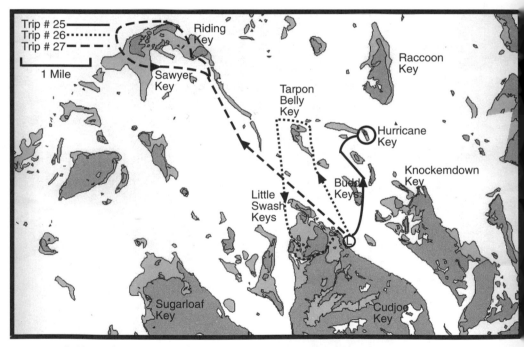

3.12. Cudjoe Key Area: Trips # 25–27

Trip # 25

Birding through the Budd Keys to Hurricane Key

Launch Site: MM 21.5 (bayside) onto Blimp Road on Cudjoe Key
Location: Across Kemp Channel, through the Budd Keys, and around tiny Hurricane Key
Paddling Time: 2 hours
Comments: Backcountry paddle through mangrove keys teeming with bird life including magnificent frigate birds.
Note: Consult a field guide for specific species' range and season. Peak migration is in mid-October. Birding is usually best in winter and early spring.

North and east of Cudjoe Key lie three island groups particularly rich in avian treasures. The Budd Keys, Hurricane Key, and Tarpon Belly Key can all be reached from the boat ramp on Kemp Channel. It would take more than four hours to make a swing through all of them, but if you're carrying binoculars and a Bird Life List with you, you'll want to split the trip into segments. One good option is to paddle through the Budd Keys and around Hurricane Key.

Launch from the boat ramp at the end of Blimp Road on Cudjoe Key. As you enter Kemp Channel from the launch site, you'll see a small mangrove islet lying halfway between Cudjoe and Knockemdown Keys. Skirt the western edge of this island, heading northwest (left) for the first of the Budd Keys. As you paddle, you'll pass Fat Albert the surveillance blimp's base. It's interesting to watch the flurry of activity that accompanies the launching or grounding of the huge airship, and this is the closet look you'll get, as the base is closed to visitors. Another great view as you paddle toward the Budds is underneath you. The hardbottom seafloor is covered with huge loggerhead sponges.

After about a half hour of paddling you'll reach the southern tip of the first Budd Key. An old dock just west of here marks the site of an abandoned homestead complete with coconut palms. Bear to your right along the key's eastern shore. Three islands make up the Budd Key group; the

Seasons in the Florida Keys can seem out of sync with the rest of the United States. While most Americans take their vacations in summer, peak season here is winter—not only for humans but for birds as well. The migration of birds heading south for the winter starts with shore-birds returning in July and August. From August to December song-birds make the trip, and raptors and waterfowl follow shortly thereafter. Some species of these migratory visitors begin leaving the keys in late February; the songbirds stay until May. Ospreys, bald eagles, magnificent frigate birds, mangrove cuckoos, white-crowned pigeons, collared doves, and other species—including naturalized parrots on the lam from their cages—are year-round residents. The backcountry is Birdland.

southern two lie across from each other, while the third rests just north of them at the apex of their triangular layout. There is rich bird and marine life within their sheltered perimeter. Wading birds feed in the shallow water, and ospreys nest on the stouter mangroves, often perilously close to the tide line. If you look high, high up into the sky, you might see an eagle, as I have several times here, or perhaps a very distinctive, very large, very black bird.

There is a reason why magnificent frigate birds are called magnificent, a reason you'll know when you see these jet black birds, wings expanded more than seven and a half feet, kitelike against a cobalt blue sky. They nest west of Key West but are most often seen gliding over backcountry waters. Their silhouettes are elegant—slim bodies with broad wings, long hooked silver bills, and deeply forked tails. Males are all black, while females have white breasts. Males also have a brilliant red pouch under their throats which they inflate when they are near their nests. Great flyers and gliders, they are inept fishers. When they near other birds, you'll hear a storm of protest, for frigate birds feed themselves and their young by stealing from other birds, forcing seabirds to disgorge their catch in midair.

From the apex of the Budd Keys triangle you can see little Hurricane Key on your right (northeast). You can paddle up and around it in about a half hour. Ironically, Hurricane Key survived Hurricane Georges in fine shape. Its mangroves are deep green, and the ospreys that nest there are doting parents who will take turns wheeling and diving toward anyone they need to ward away from their home. On the far side of the island, away from the ospreys, you can tie up your kayak and splash around in the water amid schools of green baitfish and mangrove snappers.

Paddling back south through the Budd Keys will give you another chance to get out the binoculars and field guide. You won't need binoculars to see the boat launch across Kemp Channel, past Fat Albert on Cudjoe Key.

Trip # 26

Tarpon Belly Key and the Little Swash Keys

Launch Site: MM 21.5 (bayside) onto Blimp Road on Cudjoe Key
Location: Tarpon Belly Key north of Cudjoe Key
Paddling Time: 3 hours
Comments: Moderately taxing paddle up a wide channel to a group of islands with a sandy beach.
Note: The tides pour in through Kemp Channel, making paddling against them an endurance trial. Then again, paddling with the tide here makes you feel quite talented. Check the tide table before heading out.

The launch site for reaching Tarpon Belly is the same one used for trips # 24 and # 25. You'll find it by turning onto Blimp Road from the bayside of U.S. 1 at MM 21.5. After you've unloaded your gear at the dead end of Blimp Road and parked off to the side away from the boat ramp, you can see how the tide is running through Kemp Channel and whether the wind is up. You'll be paddling straight out Kemp Channel almost six miles round-trip, and there are two other, more sheltered trips you can take from this same launch site.

If the weather's cooperating, push off from the ramp and head to your left (north) in a diagonal across the channel for the southernmost Budd Key. From here you'll parallel the western shore of this island before striking off northwest across a wide body of water dotted with shoals. You'll

There's a beach on the biggest island in the Tarpon Belly Keys, and its gleaming whiteness can be seen from a great distance. It looks very much like a tarpon belly. Vestiges of human habitation on the island are a reminder of what these keys would be like today if it weren't for their status as wildlife refuges. There's good fishing in the flats en route to Tarpon Belly, so pack a rod and reel and a Florida fishing license if you're so inclined.

see the other two Budd Keys emerge on your right, followed by Hurricane Key. Within a half hour you'll reach the back side of Tarpon Belly Key. This is not its best profile. There are several signs of past human habitation—broken-down bridges, pieces of rusting steel. The establishment of the Great White Heron National Wildlife Refuge turned this and other backcountry islands over to their original owners—cormorants and ospreys, ibis, egrets, and herons.

Tarpon Belly's beach is on its western shore. It's rocky, not sandy, and the trees here are nonindigenous Australian pines. Still, in the Keys any beach is a rarity, and one with shade is even rarer and more desirable. Australian pines looked like a good thing to the people who imported them, but park rangers have recently declared open warfare on them. The pines, actually members of the casuarina family, are known as "she-oaks" and "horsetail trees." They can grow to be a hundred feet tall, and they do create a sort of wispy shade. Unfortunately they also produce a toxin that kills off any vegetation trying to grow around them. They are subject to blow-downs in hurricanes and even lesser winds because their great height above the ground is not matched by a strong root system beneath it. Efforts to eradicate Australian pines entail chopping and burning the trees, a tricky thing given Florida's recent drought. It will probably take many decades to reduce their grip on Keys beaches.

Working your way counterclockwise around the main key and its neighboring islets will probably rustle the feathers of cormorants and wading birds. When you're ready to wing it yourself, head back across Kemp Channel. If you have the time, a side trip to the Little Swash Keys off the northern tip of Cudjoe Key provides pleasant paddling in skinny water. It's easiest to work your way along the outer edge of these tiny islets from north to south and then head back up between them and the shore of Cudjoe Key, passing through a nice basin along the way. There are plenty of nooks and crannies to explore in the Little Swash Keys, but you may have to scoot your boat through some very thin water to do it. You'll be rewarded with views of Fat Albert and plenty of backcountry creatures.

You can then work your way down Cudjoe's eastern shore, getting a final close-up view of the blimp base en route back to the launch site.

Trip # 27

Riding Key and Sawyer Key

Launch Site: MM 21.5 (bayside) onto Blimp Road on Cudjoe Key
Paddling Time: 5½ hours
Comments: All-day paddle through unsheltered water to two beautiful keys with extensive shoals and sandbars.
Note: This trip can be very tiring and should be taken only if you're confident of your kayaking and orienteering ability. Bring a kayaking partner, a compass, a chart, two pocket flares, at least two gallons of water per person, an anchor, a rope, a hat, and plenty of sunscreen. Let someone know where you're going and when you expect to be back. Do not take this trip if small-craft warnings are posted. Watch the sky for thunderstorms, lightning, and waterspouts. Return to the nearest shore immediately if these conditions threaten.

On sunny days you used to be able to stand on the boat ramp at the end of Blimp Road on Cudjoe Key, look to the northwest, and see a shiny piece of metal flashing like a beacon. It was very far away—the farthest thing on the horizon—yet I never saw it without feeling drawn there, and I paddled there many times. Recently the U.S. Fish and Wildlife Service demolished the source of that shiny beacon, the roof of a geodesic dome house on Sawyer Key. It's harder now to spot this destination from the boat launch, but "flashy" doesn't always mean "better," and it's much better for the creatures of the backcountry now that people don't live there.

Making the trip out to Sawyer Key requires the proper conditions. First, you need five hours of daylight. Then you need winds under twelve knots, and tides that you won't have to battle on either leg of the trip. Finding these conditions in winter can be tough. Spring and summer hold better possibilities, but intense heat can build up then, and lightning can flare up in the rainy season's thundershowers. So keep this trip in the back of your mind until the right day comes along. It will be worth the wait.

To reach the launch site, turn bayside off U.S. 1 at MM 21.5 onto Blimp Road. Keep going straight, past the road that leads off left to the blimp base. Park at the end of the road, away from the boat launch. Before you push off, look to your left out to the most distant key on the horizon. It's just a speck. Are you ready?

Launch your kayak and work your way north up Cudjoe Key's eastern shore, then on past the Little Swash Keys. If wind and tide aren't a problem, you can stay in the middle of Kemp Channel. It will take about an hour of steady paddling for you to draw parallel with Tarpon Belly Key. If you're tired, head east to Tarpon Belly's beach and take a break off its shore—it's the last land you'll see until beachless Riding Key.

If you don't need to stop, keep to the west (left) of Tarpon Belly on a course for Riding Key in deep (six- to twenty-one-foot) water. Two thin sandbars ribbon this area. They begin with beautiful healthy seagrass beds, which give way to a sandy bottom composed of tiny coral fragments and the skeletal remains of marine cacti. This is a nice place to anchor up and take a swim or hoist a dive flag and tow your kayak as you swim along with a "swim rope." You can remain in this shallow water almost all the way to Riding Key or break away from it if it gets too skinny to paddle in easily.

Once you've reached Riding Key, follow its southern and western shores in shallow water on a course for the southeastern tip of Sawyer Key. Sawyer is shaped like a rib cage, with two fairly symmetrical main islands protecting its heart—a small group of islets just to the south. The northern shore of the island lies at the edge of the Gulf of Mexico. The coastline here is surprisingly rocky, the remnants of an ancient reef. Whitecaps break loudly here and the tide pours in. The water offshore is deep in places, and it can turn a very un-Keys-like jade green. A paddle around this shore can be quite interesting, but it can be dangerous when the wind and tide are up. Jagged coral capable of slicing through your hull pokes out of the water here, so explore this northern shore only on calm days. A beach lies on Sawyer's northwestern shore, and there is good snorkeling in the water just off it.

Farther along the western shore you'll pass the homestead that used to be here. Then as you round the western shore and turn back south toward Cudjoe Basin, a huge sandbar opens up. On a sunny day it's as if a floodlight has been turned on a stage set with every imaginable shade of blue, turquoise, aqua, and white. The shallow waters here pulse with color, and thousands of tiny baitfish explode around you as you paddle. Sharks glide beneath your boat. Houndfish rise and scoot across the water on their backfins. The seascape seems electric, it's so bright.

Tiny green mangrove islets dot these sheltered southern waters. If you've admired pictures of South Sea Islands, you'll do a double-take here. Portions of this area are closed to boat traffic, so be sure to respect the regulations set up to protect native bird populations. But having paddled so far, do linger and admire the view.

When it's time to head back, look for Fat Albert's white balloon shape flying high above Cudjoe Key. You're far from the roadbound keys here, and the Earth's curvature makes for whimsical changes in what usually looks so solid. Here and there you'll see tiny strands of land. The closest one on your left is green, and to its right lies another tiny green head. Straight ahead you'll see white dots on a green background, then what looks like a tiny pink triangle, then more white dots. As you paddle, the view will become less impressionistic with each stroke and with each of the 120 minutes the return trip takes. You'll recognize what you saw as the length of Tarpon Belly Key and the Budd Keys just past them. The leftmost dot shows itself to be Fat Albert's base; the pink pile, a landfill mound on Sugarloaf Key; the other white dots, houses near Bow Channel, separating Cudjoe from Sugarloaf Key.

From the edge of the Gulf in shimmering heat the Keys look like pearls spilled on a piece of aqua satin. Distance truly can improve a view.

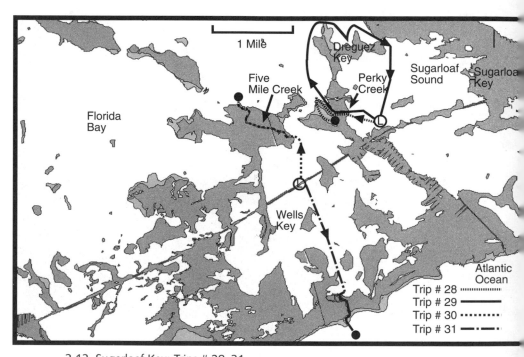

3.13. Sugarloaf Key: Trips # 28–31

Trip # 28

Perky Creek

Launch Site: MM 17 (bayside), Sugarloaf Marina
Location: Perky Creek on Lower Sugarloaf Key
Paddling Time: 1 hour round-trip through Perky Creek, ½ hour more to explore south of it
Comments: Pretty, easy paddle through a narrow, winding mangrove creek.
Note: Kayak rentals available at Sugarloaf Marina, (305) 745-3135; reservations advisable for holidays and spring break.

There's no place like a sheltered mangrove creek when northerly winds blow or the sun beats down too strongly. This pretty little creek has the added advantage of being close to both Key West and Big Pine Key. Kayak rentals are available at the launch site, and there's even a one-of-a-kind bat tower nearby.

Both the creek and the tower are named for Florida real estate developer R. C. Perky, who bought Sugarloaf Key just before World War I. Mosquitoes blanketed the Keys back then, turning white clapboard houses black with their swarms. Perky became convinced, after reading a book entitled *Bats, Mosquitoes and Dollars,* that the secret to thwarting mosquitoes lay in attracting bats, which reputedly feasted on the insects. He sent off for plans to build a thirty-five-foot tower that, equipped with the right bait, would attract and house thousands of bats. The bat tower has stood for more than seventy years at the end of a little road next to the creek and Sugarloaf Marina. No bat has ever visited it, but many people have, admiring its unique architecture and cypress gingerbread trim. It's an odd little thing—a glorified, quirky birdhouse.

6. Perky's Bat Tower, Sugarloaf Key

You can see Perky's Bat Tower as you paddle across Sugarloaf Sound to the entrance of Perky Creek. To reach the launch site, turn into Sugarloaf Lodge on the bayside of U.S. 1 at MM 17. Behind the lodge is a marina. For a dollar you can launch from their boat ramp. You'll see the brown wooden bat tower on your left as you paddle northwest across Sugarloaf

Sound. The entrance to Perky Creek can be hard to spot, so keep a close eye on the shoreline for an opening. It's located midway between the bat tower and the first point projecting from the peninsula on your left. You'll know you've missed it if a much wider boat channel opens up on the left. Work your way back down to the creek if you don't want to play tag with powerboats in the channel.

The creek is a solace—swift and deep, with sheaves of turtle grass waving up green from the bottom. It's narrow and protected, with mangroves obscuring the water's path in spots. Barely a kayak's width sometimes, it demonstrates the backcountry's diversity, offering open marine views reminiscent of the Caribbean but also intimate waterways resembling Louisiana bayous. The flow of water through the creek will usually show you which way to turn as you work your way through the mangrove maze toward more open water off the peninsula's western shore. An outgoing tide can push the water through here very quickly. This isn't dangerous, but it can make you feel like you're piloting a bumper-kayak. If your paddle pulls apart, dismantle it and use it canoe-style to propel your boat and fend off vegetation. This can be challenging and lots of fun, and I often time my trips to enjoy the short, wild ride. Then again, working against an incoming tide can feel like a pitched battle—don't try it with a friend or small child you've been trying to convert to kayaking.

Perky Creek empties into a boat channel that, if you bear left (northwest), soon gives onto a shallow-water basin. Egrets and herons abound in the waters to the south of the channel, and there are plenty of tidepools to explore. Boat traffic here is virtually nonexistent. Following the shore to the north (right) of the channel will put you on a course to Dreguez Key (described in trip # 29). This area is frequented by flats fishermen and zipped across by powerboaters using one of two channels cutting through between the marina and the Narrows.

So you have lots of options—north, south, or back through Perky Creek with its underwater aquarium of gray snappers and its twists and turns.

Trip # 29

Up and around Upper Sugarloaf Sound

Launch Site: MM17 (bayside), Sugarloaf Marina
Location: Perky Creek, Dreguez Key, and environs
Paddling Time: 3 hours
Comments: Everything the backcountry has to offer on one trip—a mangrove creek, sandy shoals, and circumnavigation of a pretty key
Note: Kayak rentals available at Sugarloaf Marina, (305) 745-3135; reservations advisable for holidays and spring break. Circumnavigating Dreguez Key is impossible during extreme low tides, when beautiful but impassable sandbars ring the island's eastern shore.

The launch site for this trip is Sugarloaf Marina on the bayside of U.S. 1 at MM 17. It costs a dollar to launch your kayak from here, but there's great parking, an easy launch, bathrooms, and a small store. As you push off, look to your left across the lower section of Upper Sugarloaf Sound. You'll see a brown wooden structure that resembles a Dutch windmill without blades—it's Perky's Bat Tower (see trip # 28). The entrance to

---

Maybe you can find the bomb holes. They were created by fighter jets dropping loads of live ammunition all over backcountry waters in the 1950s. They're not marked on any nautical charts, and it's unlikely anyone will tell you exactly where they are. Some very nice bomb holes can be found on this trip. How nice can a bomb hole be? you wonder. Very nice indeed, if you want a deep snorkeling spot or a secret fishing hole. So look for the bomb holes.

This trip offers other treasures, too, because it travels through so many different backcountry habitats—a narrow, twisting mangrove creek, a white sandy shoal, several beautiful shallow bays, and a passage amid mangrove islets.

Perky Creek lies farther north along this shore, south of a much wider boat channel. Wend your way through this lovely little mangrove creek until it rejoins the boat channel. Bear right, heading out of the channel and into a wide shallow water basin.

Head north (right) along this basin's shore. You'll pass another boat channel running parallel to the one you just left. Ahead off to your left you'll see little Bill Finds Key and even smaller Marjoe Key. The western shoreline of Dreguez Key is on your right. It will take you about forty-five minutes to reach the northwestern tip of Dreguez Key, and what you find there will depend upon the tide's stage when you arrive. If the tide's out, you'll be welcomed by a gorgeous white sand beach. Wading birds will fill the flats offshore, probing for dinner in the marly mud. The entire northern shore of Sugarloaf Key will be dressed in glistening sand. And the route ahead will be impassable; you will have to turn around and retrace your trip back to the marina.

If the tide is in, you probably won't even know there's a shoal here. Still, this is a beautiful spot to rest and take in the impressive backcountry panorama in front of you, with the large Snipe Keys sprawling west through Turkey Basin and the myriad little green Barracuda Keys poised on the horizon at the Gulf of Mexico's edge. With plenty of water under your hull you can begin working your way east (right) along Dreguez's northern shore. Green mangroves are everywhere here, and from the low vantage point of your kayak you won't be able to tell a continuous landmass from a group of islands. If you want to keep surprises to a minimum, keep the bulk of Dreguez Key on your right as you paddle south down the key's eastern shore. Three radio towers will eventually rise out of this vast greenery—they're located by Bow Channel on Sugarloaf Key. Aim for the one that most closely resembles the Eiffel Tower and you'll soon see the small key that lies astride the southern portion of Upper Sugarloaf Sound. You'll also see the distinctive red and white roof of Sugarloaf Marina resting alongside U.S. 1. This is your takeout point.

Trip # 30

Five Mile Creek

Launch Site: MM 16 (bayside)
Location: Five Mile Creek in the Saddlebunch Keys
Paddling Time: 1½ hours
Comments: Fish-filled tidal creek with "secret tunnels" and good vistas over Turkey Basin

To reach the launch site, park along the bayside of U.S. 1 near MM 16. The gravel shoulder is wide here, and there is a visible break in the low mangroves that line the shore. You can use the rocks near the launch site to keep your feet dry as you board your kayak. As you head out you'll see the long, unbroken shore of an unnamed island. The entrance to Five Mile Creek, which is marked on charts, is located at the southeastern corner of this key. To reach it, head north across the basin and bear right (east) when you reach the southernmost tip of the key. It takes about fifteen minutes from launching until you notice the creek's current riffling the basin's water. A homemade "channel marker" of plastic pipe stands near the creek's mouth.

Five Mile Creek isn't five miles long, but it's much wider than Perky Creek less than a mile to the southeast. The entrance contains streamers of thick green- and yellow-bladed seagrass that are particularly lovely

This is a great trip to take with a couple of friends even when the weather's not perfect. It's close to the highway, Five Mile Creek is easy to find, and you can paddle three-abreast down it. Along the way you'll see Perky's Bat Tower and two very pretty basins. Fish watchers and fishermen will be happy indeed with the abundant schools of mangrove snappers, as well as permits, bonefish, sheepshead, and houndfish. Kids love the tunnels.

when sunlight plays on the water. Here and there the creek widens into little lagoons that look like stocked aquariums. The water here is deep, and you may be tempted to jump in for a swim or snorkel. Be forewarned: powerboaters zip through this winding creek en route to Sugarloaf Marina. They may not have time to slow down or even notice a dive flag. It's far safer to get in the water along the shore of Turkey Basin.

Small "secret" mangrove tunnels break off from the main creek on both sides. While they're all dead ends, they can be fun to explore, especially if your party includes children. Look for elegant endangered tree snails and crabs climbing the mangrove branches. Be careful of the brilliant orange fire sponges growing just below the waterline on the mangroves' prop roots, though. They can burn your skin if you touch them.

After several twists and turns the creek empties into Turkey Basin. The mouth of the creek is an excellent place to watch the sunset on summer days when light lingers well after the sun itself has vanished. On blustery days it's a good spot to moor up among mangrove branches for conversation and snacks. The shoreline stretching east and west offers nice birdwatching and snorkel spots, although the view west is marred by a line of navy communication towers.

Your return route can wind back through Five Mile Creek into Lower Sugarloaf Sound or bear right along the eastern and southern shores of the unnamed key you've just traversed. Let wind, tide, and desire guide your choice.

Trip # 31

Sugarloaf Creek

Launch Site: MM 16 (oceanside)
Location: Sugarloaf Creek on Lower Sugarloaf Key
Paddling Time: 2 hours
Comments: Paddle through a tidal creek that empties into the Atlantic Ocean.

Note: Crossing the shallow-water basin north of Sugarloaf Creek can be difficult in strong southerly winds or at low tide.

Sugarloaf Creek has high banks and good fishing. It's a nice way to enter the ocean, but there's no public access to it from the nearest road, the end of Sugarloaf Beach Road. You can get there by kayak, though, if you pull off U.S. 1 at MM 16 (oceanside). Park your car on the gravel shoulder and then portage your boat and gear down the steep embankment marked by huge concrete pilings used to carry the electric lines feeding Key West and the Lower Keys. You'll see a break in the mangroves near a few of these pilings. You can launch your boat from here.

The real estate boom of the 1960s and 1970s brought uninterrupted carloads of sun worshippers to the Lower Keys, and many of them ended up building pastel-hued cement houses along canals dredged to provide easy access to the Atlantic Ocean. Both Upper and Lower Sugarloaf Keys have subdivisions full of such homes. When brakes were applied to the go-go real estate caravan, a few areas somehow remained unbuilt. Usually these areas were bounded by undredgeable shoals or were overwash islands routinely flooded. Occasionally prime properties, like the north end of Upper Sugarloaf Key, were forced off the market by federal legislation. A high concentration of these non-properties also exists today between Sugarloaf and the Saddlebunch Keys.

This lesson in economic geography may help you make sense of the landscape as you launch your boat and head south from U.S. 1 toward Sugarloaf Creek. You'll be paddling across skinny water through Lower Sugarloaf Sound. Take a good look at the tall, scraggly, dull gray-green Australian pines on the distant shore ahead of you. They lie along Sugarloaf Beach, just east of the creek's mouth. Take a look behind you too, noting which piling you're parked by. You won't be able to see your car on your return to the launch site, because the roadbed is much higher than the water here.

Once you launch, to your left and right you'll see cement houses, often with cement lawns, next to cement canals—each house with at least one boat. Quintessential South Florida. But ahead as you paddle you'll see green, uninhabited Wells Key, and en route you'll pass over a healthy hardbottom seafloor rich in sponges. Within fifteen minutes you'll reach

Wells Key. The squawks of wading birds will likely drown out any lingering traffic noise. Here the journey begins in earnest. Keeping your aim fixed on the line of distant trees, paddle south toward two small islands.

A white channel marker will come into view on your right. The water deepens here, marking the lush mangrove delta of Sugarloaf Creek. The creek offers shelter from any winds that may have whipped up Sugarloaf Sound. It's a good spot to picnic, fish, or relax. Traveling south, you'll pass under the Sugarloaf Road bridge and emerge just to the west of the Sammy family's oceanside homestead. High-priced homes extend eastward from here along Sugarloaf Beach. To the west, however, a large tract of land is held in trust by the Nature Conservancy. And the ocean out front, dotted with patch reefs a quarter mile offshore (see trip # 32), belongs to us all.

Trip # 32

Patch Reef Bonanza Shuttle Trip: Sugarloaf Key to Geiger Key

Launch Sites: MM 16 (oceanside), and MM 10.8 (oceanside) onto Boca Chica Road and then Geiger Road
Location: Sugarloaf Key to Geiger Key
Paddling Time: 4½ hours
Comments: Daylong shuttle trip requiring one car parked at MM 16 and another at the Geiger Key Marina. Paddle across Sugarloaf Sound, along the Atlantic Ocean—with stops at three patch reefs—and through Geiger Channel.
Note: This is an ambitious trip that requires stamina, kayaking experi-

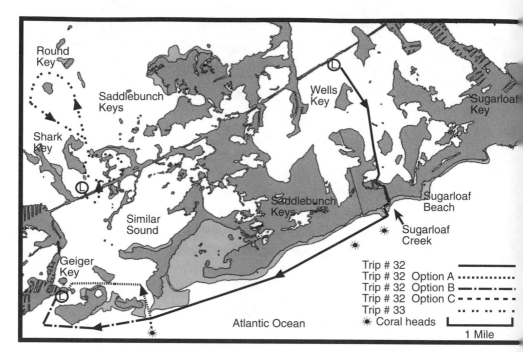

3.14. Sugarloaf, Geiger, and Saddlebunch Keys: Trips # 32–33

ence, proper timing, and favorable weather conditions. To enjoy the trip best, gauge your trip to coincide with an outgoing tide. This way you will not fight the water as you head out to sea. There are no mooring buoys at the three patch reefs, which are in water more than fifteen feet deep. Bring at least one snorkeling partner, a gallon of water per person, an anchor, a dive flag, and a length of strong rope. Be very careful to anchor in a sandy patch of seafloor. Never anchor on coral. Practice getting out of and back into your kayak in deep water before you take this trip. Do not take this trip if small-craft warnings are posted. Watch the sky for thunderstorms, lightning, and waterspouts. Return to shore immediately if these conditions threaten. Do not take this trip if you are unsure of your paddling, swimming, or snorkeling ability or your ability to pull yourself into your kayak from deep water.

Begin by parking one car at the public boat ramp next to Geiger Key Marina. To reach it, turn toward the ocean at MM 10.8 onto Boca Chica Road. Follow this to Geiger Road and turn left. The public boat ramp is on the right, just past the Geiger Key Marina. Drive your other car up U.S. 1 to MM 16 (oceanside) and park on the wide gravel shoulder there. Carry your gear down the embankment to one of several clearings in the mangroves that line the water's edge.

If the tide is falling, it will help to push you out across Lower Sugarloaf Sound. Paddle past Wells Key with your eyes on the feathery dull green Australian pines on the horizon. Keep heading south across the sound, past two small mangrove islands. Soon the white channel marker for Sugarloaf Creek will appear on your right. Follow it through the winding creek itself. Within an hour after launching from U.S. 1 you'll pass under Sugarloaf Beach Road and emerge into the Atlantic Ocean.

A shoal runs along the coastline here, and you may have to pick your way through the channel to cross it. Keep heading out to sea for fifteen minutes or so, then head west down the green expanse of the key. Some of this land belongs to the U.S. Fish and Wildlife Service, and more has recently been acquired by the Nature Conservancy. Cars used to hum along the old roadbed of U.S. 1 here; now the area is strictly for the birds. The

---

Got two cars with kayak racks? Want to see what's under the sea? Then start checking those tide tables and praying for sunny, calm weather. Spring and fall are the best times to take this trip, although summer's good if you leave early in the morning before the heat gets too intense. The first body of water you'll paddle through is covered in trip # 31 (Sugarloaf Creek). The last section is covered in trip # 36 (Geiger Coral Heads) and trip # 34 (Similar Sound). Study the more detailed descriptions of these trips and look at your NOAA chart before heading out. Every leg of this trip is enjoyable in its own right, but strung together they make for a fabulous day on the water. Since you'll paddle for more than four hours, make sure that you plan on dedicating a whole day to this trip—you'll need it to enjoy time under the water as well as on it. Remember that the four-and-a-half-hour paddling time is just that—it doesn't include snorkeling or resting time.

mangroves are festooned with ibis, herons, egrets, and pelicans. Song-birds dart through the undergrowth and short-tailed hawks, known locally as klee-klees, soar above the old roadbed searching for mice and other small prey.

More natural treasures can be found just offshore. About five hundred yards west of the last, white house on Sugarloaf Beach and five to seven hundred feet offshore (a fifteen-minute paddle), dark brown splotches appear beneath the turquoise water—the first of many patch reefs that run between Sugarloaf Creek and Geiger Key Boat Channel. By now you should be ready for a swim. Find a sandy spot to anchor in, moor your boat together with your partner's, secure your hatches, and raise a dive flag. Take turns with your dive partner, each exploring the patch reef alone. Once you have both successfully gotten out of and back into your kayak, you can enjoy the view together.

Substantial brain corals grow from the ocean floor here, beautiful in themselves and home to many Technicolored reef fish. Tiny neon gobies are only an inch and a half long, yet their jet black bodies seem to pulsate with an electric blue band running from eye to caudal fin. Spiny urchins poke out from the coral—don't touch, but do admire the contrasting textures of their irregular long black spikes against the brain coral's smooth white ribbons. It's quite a study in design. Listen, too. It's possible to hear rainbow parrotfish nibbling on the algae that coats the coral heads.

Take your time enjoying these and other citizens of the reef. Take time above water, too, to reapply sunscreen and drink plenty of fresh water. When you're ready to push off, haul anchor and resume paddling west. Five minutes from your last snorkeling spot you'll find another. This patch reef is closer to the surface, and I have even seen its grooved brown flank exposed above the waves. Be careful to anchor away from it in a sandy spot. Doing otherwise will damage both the coral and your hull. Again, take turns with your dive partner exploring the reef alone until you're sure that you can get out of and back into your kayak safely. You still have a long paddle, and another patch reef, ahead of you. If you're tired, rest awhile or head back through Sugarloaf Creek to the launch site at MM 16.

If you're ready to continue toward Geiger Key, start paddling west again. The water here off the shore of Saddlebunch Key is home to sea turtles, eagle rays, and dolphins. All make great traveling companions as you paddle along. If the tide is still streaming out, you may have to go farther into the ocean to avoid the shoals that extend out from the shoreline. Sometimes the shoals here look like thin grassy meadows. But instead of cows grazing, wading birds bend their long necks to the matted sea bottom for tiny fish and crustaceans.

It will take almost an hour to cross the expanse of Saddlebunch Key and its wide bay. Then, as you reach the mouth of Shark Channel, you will have some choices to consider.

Option A: If there's still plenty of water nearshore you could forgo a trip to the third patch reef altogether and return to the takeout site at Geiger Key by a shorter route. You can shave off about thirty minutes' paddling by heading into Similar Sound via Shark Channel. You would pass between Pelican Key on your left and Saddlebunch Key on your right, then make your way west between Saddlehill Key (left) and Bird Key (right). When you reach the eastern shore of Geiger Key, you'll see the end of Geiger Road and, just to its left, a white house marking the end of the boat channel into Geiger Key Marina. By following this small channel west for a few hundred yards, you'll reach the public boat ramp where you parked your first car.

Option B: This is not an option but a necessity if the water nearshore has gotten "skinny." Keep paddling west across Shark Channel, then along Pelican Key and Saddlehill Key until you see the channel markers and homemade sign for Geiger Key Marina. This route is longer, but it has the advantage of being a no-brainer at a time when you may be tired and happy to keep things simple. You'll have plenty of water under your hull and a well-marked channel running from the western edge of Saddlehill Key directly to Geiger Key Marina—with its copious beer and bathrooms.

Option C: This option can easily be combined with either of the first two. Before heading back to the launch site via either Shark Channel or Geiger

Key Boat Channel, paddle out into the ocean for fifteen minutes beginning from the eastern edge of Pelican Key to the Geiger coral heads described in trip # 36. Savor one last visit to the incredible patch reefs of the
Lower Keys. Then head back to shore.

You may want to stop off for a meal or a drink at the Geiger Key Marina after loading up the first of your two shuttle cars. The mood here is
relaxed, with an outdoor tiki bar overlooking the mangroves and a small
stage for live music on weekends. The marina's little campground is very
popular in season, but this is a locals' place first and foremost, with none
of the studied tourist look found in fancy resorts. It's known as "the back-
side of Paradise."

Trip # 33

Skinny-Water Kayaking in the Saddlebunches

Launch Site: MM 11 (oceanside) at Shark Key boat ramp
Location: Shark Key and the northern Saddlebunch Keys
Paddling Time: 30 minutes to 2 hours
Comments: Kayaking in water often less than a foot in depth through a
maze of backcountry islets.
Note: Check a tide table before launching so that you'll have enough wa-
ter to float your boat.

Destinations are not always necessary, and the Saddlebunches provide a
perfect place to take a short break from life on land. I go there to think or
watch the clouds. The sky seems bigger here somehow.

It's also a good place to practice standing up in your kayak. Plastic sit-
upon kayaks bear more than a passing resemblance to fat surfboards—
except, of course, that they're concave where the seat is hollowed out. You
won't want to stand up on them to ride waves, although sitting down and
doing so is exciting. There probably is no real reason for standing up in a

〰〰〰〰〰〰〰〰

> It doesn't get any simpler than this. First there's the launch site, a nice new public boat ramp just over ten miles from Key West. Then there's the scenery, a maze of mangrove islets opening up to panoramic views of Waltz Key Basin, perfect for sunset viewing. And forget about boat traffic—the water here is far too shallow for anything but a kayak.
>
> There is no real destination on this trip. You could paddle along the eastern shore of ritzy Shark Key, admiring the luxury homes there, or the wilder shore of neighboring O'Hara Key before striking off to the north up and around Round Key. As you head back toward U.S. 1, you'll find several openings into a small lagoon often frequented by rays and wading birds. The water here is protected from strong winds.

kayak other than that it's fun. It's harder than standing up on a surfboard or Windsurfer because it's tippier. I get the best results by crouching on the hatch just in front of my seat and holding my paddle the way a tight-rope walker uses a pole for balance. As I rise up to full height, I step forward a tiny bit with my left foot. If I haven't fallen into the water with a splash resembling that of a leaping eagle ray, I'm usually good in this position for a couple of minutes. From this vantage point I can see (at a savings of several hundred dollars) what the flats fishermen and their clients see—game fish cruising through the shallows. Casting from this position is next to impossible, so if you plan on fishing, let your companion spot for you while you blind cast from a seated position or stand up and use a pole like flats guides do. You can also wade into these shallow hard-bottom flats to fish.

Whether sit-upon kayak fishing will ever win popularity as a crossover sport is anyone's guess. But if sports historians go looking for its birthplace, they're bound to find it here in the Saddlebunches.

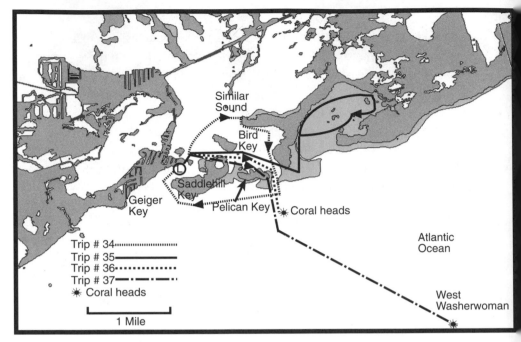

3.15. Geiger Key: Trips # 34–37

Trip # 34

Similar Sound

Launch Site: MM 10.8 (oceanside) onto Boca Chica Road, then Geiger Road

Location: Similar Sound, off Geiger Key

Paddling Time: 2 hours

Comments: Leisurely loop trip through protected waters and along the Atlantic Ocean.

Note: You can delete the ocean paddle portion of this trip, staying completely within Similar Sound.

If you like combining your kayaking with live music, beer, and barbecue, take this trip on Sunday afternoon, when Geiger Key Marina hosts a live band. If you like your kayaking with a side order of sunset, take it any day of the year. The clouds here can blossom to spectacular size, especially in the summer, and when they're mauve edged in gold, they fit my friend's nickname for them—"children's Bible clouds." In truth, this trip is enjoyable anytime, any day, with the possible exception of when the Naval Air Station revs its test engines or conducts flight training. Of course, if you're an aviation buff, this could be a plus.

To reach the launch site, turn oceanside off U.S. 1 at MM 10.8 onto Boca Chica Road. Follow this road until you see a small sign for Geiger Key Marina, turning left onto Geiger Road. Turn right just past the marina, and launch from the public boat ramp. (You can also unload your boat directly onto Similar Sound at the end of Geiger Road, but because this is navy property, you may not be allowed to park there.) After pushing off, head left down the canal to where it joins Similar Sound. You will see the end of Geiger Road just past the last house along the canal.

Across the sound to the northeast you will see part of Saddlebunch Key jutting out into the water. Head for this spot. En route you'll spot a tiny inlet carved into the peninsula. This makes a good windbreak and a nice resting spot. It's deep enough for a quick swim, too. Farther north of this spot you'll see where the old section of U.S. 1 abruptly ended. You can tie up your kayak here and explore the old roadbed a bit. I call this area Lightbulb Key because, for some strange reason, every time I've visited it there have been dozens of used lightbulbs littering the ground here, all unbroken. Cars stopped traveling this road when new bridges were built to the north. Nature has been busy reclaiming the area ever since. Today it is covered with native vegetation, and a few remnants of domestic gardens, and is becoming a new habitat for birds and other creatures.

From here you can work your way along the southern shore of Similar Sound or head directly for Pelican Key, which lies on the edge of the Atlantic Ocean on the west side of Shark Channel. The northern shore of

Pelican Key is quite shallow, and it hosts an amazing array of loggerhead and vase sponges. Heading along the key's eastern shore will expose you to the boat traffic in Shark Channel, but it will also give you your first view of the ocean. You can savor this view for a half hour as you paddle along the southern shore of Pelican and then Saddlehill Key. At high tide you can pass between Pelican and Saddlehill Key and reenter Similar Sound. A shoal blocks this route at other times.

Saddlehill Key's shores had been covered with mangroves all the way to the water's edge before Hurricane Georges raked the area in the fall of 1998. The water coughed up torn seagrass which lodged in the mangroves' prop roots, stinking to high heaven. Plastic bags and fishing floats and marine flotsam and jetsam by the ton also washed up, most of it unpicturesque. Volunteers have since pulled most of this mess from the tangled roots and restored the area's beauty. But what also washed up and stayed in places where it had never stayed before was sand. Saddlehill Key got a brand-new Atlantic beach, albeit one often unapproachable and somewhat smelly. Beaches throughout the Keys fared differently in the hurricane. Sombrero Beach in Marathon grew in size and beauty, while poor Bahia Honda was almost completely washed away. Boca Chica Beach got a real sand beach, while Smathers Beach in Key West had to be rebuilt. Similar changes will occur with future storms.

By the time you reach the western edge of Saddlehill Key, you'll have a good view of Boca Chica Beach stretching in a white line toward Key West. You'll also see the channel markers and sign for Geiger Key Marina. Turn right here and enter the channel. As you work your way along the northern shore of Saddlehill Key, you'll see a small creek open up on the right. This is a nice resting spot, particularly if live music floats in from the bandstand at the marina. Let the sound carry you back into the channel, past the marina, and to the launch site. If you're hungry or thirsty or need a bathroom . . . it's right next door.

Trip # 35

Saddlebunch Bay

Launch Site: MM 10.8 (oceanside) onto Boca Chica Road, then Geiger Road
Location: Similar Sound off Geiger Key and the Saddlebunch Keys
Paddling Time: 4 hours
Comments: Quiet paddle to a very shallow oceanside bay known for its bird life and beautiful sunsets.
Note: This bay is marked as a shoal on nautical charts. You will need to take this trip at high tide to be able to explore the area.

To reach the launch site, turn toward the ocean at MM 10.8 onto Boca Chica Road. Follow this road until you see a small sign for the Geiger Key Marina. Turn left here onto Geiger Road. There is a public boat ramp past the marina on the right. You can also unload your boat directly on Similar Sound at the end of Geiger Road, but because this is navy property, you may not be allowed to park there. If you launch from the public

"Saddlebunch Bay" is not named on any nautical chart. In fact, this beautiful area east of Geiger Key is marked as a shoal, not a bay. But when the tide is high, it's an incredible kayaking destination. The route to the bay crosses Similar Sound, where huge sponges lie beneath crystal clear water. It passes between tiny Bird Key, festooned with pelicans, and Saddlehill Key, then past Pelican Key and around the tip of the largest Saddlebunch Key. Here you can branch off to explore a small tidal creek filled to the brim with mangrove snappers. Then the bay itself stretches before you, dotted with islets and tiny coves. The deep blue of the Atlantic Ocean provides a perfect backdrop.

ramp, head left (east) along the shore of Geiger Key until you reach the last house and see the end of Geiger Road.

Here you'll look across Similar Sound to the green expanse of Saddlebunch Key. Head east across the water, keeping Saddlehill Key on your right and tiny Bird Key on your left. The water here can be quite shallow, especially near the shore. Incredible sponges dot the seafloor. You're likely to see tarpon in season and sharks in this area, too—hence the names of nearby Shark Key and Shark Channel. Once you've passed Bird Key, you'll paddle through Shark Channel with Pelican Key on your right and the southernmost tip of Saddlebunch Key on your left. Powerboats and sailboats ply the deep water here, so keep an eye and ear out for them and head across the channel at your first opportunity.

Within a half hour of launching you'll reach the tip of Saddlebunch Key, passing between a tiny offshore islet and the main key. The view out to sea is magnificent. Work your way left down the coast of Saddlebunch. You'll soon see the entrance to a lovely tidal creek hung low with mangroves. This shady canopy is a welcome retreat from the tropical sun and a great windbreak. When you reemerge from the creek and look across the bay, you'll be able to tell whether there's sufficient water to paddle across. If you see shoals, head back across Shark Channel and explore Similar Sound (trip # 34) or head out to sea for a paddle or patch-reef snorkel (trip # 36). The mud in this bay is no fun to portage through.

If you've timed things correctly and the tide is high, here's your chance to be alone with nature. The farther into the bay you go, the more birds you'll see roosting in the trees and wading in the waters. Southern stingrays will whip up clouds of sand as your kayak passes over them, and sharks will race away from your boat at right angles. At the far eastern end of the bay there are several small mangrove islands. Beyond them, by noticing the height and contour of the tree line, you can tell where the old U.S. 1 roadbed once ran. On the water today there are no signs or sounds of humans in this place. Tree snails climb green mangroves in the quiet inlets and coves at the bay's far reaches as birds croak and trill and dragonflies rev their wings just above the water's surface.

After exploring the bay, you can add to this trip by heading farther east along the Atlantic shore of Saddlebunch Key. This area was recently acquired by the Nature Conservancy and constitutes an important habitat for bird and marine species. You can also add to the trip by heading west past Shark Channel, Pelican Key, and Saddlehill Key, returning to the launch site through Geiger Key Channel. Look for the channel marker sign past the western edge of Saddlehill Key. There's a small handmade "Marina" sign posted in the water. This channel can be quite busy, so be alert. The marina lies at the end of the channel, and the launch site just east of it.

Trip # 36

Geiger Coral Heads

Launch Site: MM 10.8 (oceanside) onto Boca Chica Road, then Geiger Road
Location: Patch reef off Pelican Key
Paddling Time: 1½ hours
Comments: Snorkel trip to a nearshore coral patch reef filled with tropical fish
Note: There is no mooring buoy at this site, which is located in water that is sixteen feet deep. Bring at least one snorkeling partner, an anchor, a dive flag, and a length of strong rope. Be very careful to anchor in a sandy patch of seafloor. Never anchor on coral. Practice getting out of and back into your kayak in deep water before you take this trip. Do not take this trip if small-craft warnings are posted or if you are not confident of your swimming or snorkeling ability or your ability to pull yourself into your kayak from deep water.

The coral heads are part of a series of patch reefs that run closer to shore than the main fringing reef, and are thus accessible to kayakers. While they aren't as big as the main reef frequented by dive boats, they are less crowded because they're usually overlooked by powerboaters. Yet they host the same beautiful tropical fish and coral species as the main reef. So bring an underwater camera!

To reach the launch site, turn oceanside off U.S. 1 onto Boca Chica

Summertime is dive time in the Keys. That's when water clarity is best and underwater visibility can reach more than a hundred feet. It's also when the heat is most intense and unremitting on land and when a paddle to the Geiger coral heads can be the most rewarding. Actually, this is a great destination anytime there's no strong southeast wind or threat of waterspouts or thunderstorms. In winter you may want to wear a shortie wetsuit.

Road. Follow this road until you turn left at the sign for Geiger Road. Launch from the public boat ramp on the right side of Geiger Road, just past the Geiger Key Marina. You can also unload your boat directly on Similar Sound at the end of Geiger Road, but because this is navy property, you may not be allowed to park there. If you launch from the public boat ramp, head left down the canal until you pass the last house there and enter Similar Sound. You will see the end of Geiger Road behind you.

Paddle east across the sound, keeping Saddlehill Key on your right and tiny Bird Key on your left. Then turn south and head out Shark Channel toward the Atlantic Ocean. You may encounter boat traffic in this channel, so be alert and keep to the west (right) side of the channel. Saddlebunch Key will be on your left, Pelican Key on your right. As you enter the ocean, you'll see the outline of a lighthouse far on the southeastern horizon over American Shoal on the main reef seven miles from shore.

You should head straight out to sea, aligning your boat with the eastern edge of Pelican Key. Paddle out for ten minutes. If the water's not too rumpled by wind or waves, you'll see every inch of seagrass, every sponge, every sea plume stand out clearly. Soon the water will turn a turquoise color, and dark brown mounds of brain coral will appear under your hull. Find a sandy patch and anchor your boat, mooring it together with your dive partner's boat. Never anchor on the coral itself. Raise your dive flag, make sure your hatches and paddles are secured, then take turns with your snorkeling partner exploring the water. Once you've both successfully gotten out of and back into your kayaks, enjoy the patch reef together. You'll find the usual colorful suspects here—butterfly fish, gray and French angelfish, queen and blue parrotfish, schools of yellowtail snappers, porkfish, and lots and lots of grunts. Look but don't touch the long-spined urchins or moray eels. Collect West Indian spiny lobsters only if they're in season and if you have a state lobster tag (available where fishing licenses are sold).

There are similar patch reefs farther east off Sugarloaf Beach, farther west off Boca Chica Beach, and off South Beach in Key West. All are about a ten- or fifteen-minute paddle offshore. If you'd like to paddle a bit farther out to a larger patch reef, consider trip # 37 to West Washerwoman Reef.

Trip # 37

West Washerwoman Reef

Launch Site: MM 10.8 (oceanside) onto Boca Chica Road, then Geiger Road

Location: West Washerwoman Reef off the Saddlebunch Keys (24° 33.34' N, 81° 35.03' W)

Paddling Time: 3 hours

Comments: Rewarding trip three miles out in the open ocean to a large coral patch reef.

Note: There is no mooring buoy at this site, which is located in water that is seventeen feet deep. Bring at least one snorkeling partner, a compass, an anchor, a dive flag, a length of rope, and two pocket flares. Be very careful to anchor in a sandy patch of seafloor. Never anchor on coral. Practice getting out of and back into your kayak in deep water before you take this trip. Do not take this trip if small-craft warnings are posted or if you are not confident of your paddling, swimming, or snorkeling ability or your ability to pull yourself into your kayak from deep water. Watch the sky for thunderstorms, lightning, and waterspouts. Return to shore immediately if these conditions threaten. Bring meat tenderizer and aspirin to treat (unlikely) jellyfish stings.

This should be considered an all-day trip, even though most people can paddle to and from the site in about three hours. It's a long haul over open ocean, with no shelter from sun, wind, or waves. The reward is a magical underwater realm of gaudy tropical fish, brilliant sea fans, large coral heads, sea turtles, sharks, barracudas, and more.

To reach the launch site, turn oceanside off U.S. 1 at MM 10.8 onto Boca Chica Road. Continue to Geiger Road and turn left. Park at the public boat ramp on the right-hand side of Geiger Road, just past the marina. (You can also unload your boat directly onto Similar Sound at the end of Geiger Road, but this is navy property, so you may not be able to park there.) Launch your kayak and head left down the canal until you've passed the last house and entered Similar Sound.

Head east across the sound, keeping Saddlehill Key on your right and little Bird Key on your left. Once you've passed Bird Key, head south into Shark Channel. This passes between Pelican Key on your right and Saddlebunch Key on your left. As the channel enters the ocean, you'll see the lighthouse towering above American Shoal on the main reef seven miles offshore near the southeastern horizon. West Washerwoman lies almost halfway between American Shoal and the entrance to Shark Channel. Take a moment to enjoy the view and assess the weather. It will take you an hour of steady paddling to reach the dive site and another hour to return to the channel. There are several beautiful journeys in protected waters on either side of you (trips # 34–36), so don't feel compelled to visit West Washerwoman if conditions aren't favorable or if the water visibility is poor.

If you're ready to go to sea, line up your kayak's bow with the lighthouse on American Shoal and your stern with the southeastern edge of Pelican Key on a compass heading of 130°M. As your boat rocks on the ocean's swells, scan the horizon for the day marker that stands above West Washerwoman. It is closer in and to the west of the lighthouse. This will help you to keep on course. The immensity of the ocean, especially from the vantage point of a kayak, is awe-inspiring. Behind you is the long stretch of Sugarloaf, then Pelican and Saddlehill Key, and beyond that the

Why Some People Dive Naked

It's not what you might think. Hedonism doesn't cause it, at least not between Mother's Day and Father's Day—it's the sea lice. These tiny thimble jellyfish larvae are only the size of a fleck of black pepper but, boy, do they make you itch. Carried by winds and waves from Central America via the Gulf Stream, they cause little trouble to anyone until they encounter pressure—like when they come between you and your bathing suit. This causes them to react by firing up their stinging cells, producing itchy red welts sometimes accompanied by nausea, fever, and chills.

If you're stung, remove your suit and wash the affected skin with soapy water. (Remember to wash out your suit thoroughly, too.) Topical lotions and antihistamines will soothe the pain in most cases, although severe cases may need to be treated with prescribed steroids.

Staying out of the water during the sea lice migration is a preventative option, as is eliminating the source of pressure between human skin and larval jellyfish.

Taking off your suit will not protect you from a bigger member of the jellyfish family—the dreaded Portuguese man-of-war. Usually borne on southeastern waves, these jellies are beautiful to behold— iridescent pastel blue rimmed with pink. But their long tentacles float far off from their bodies and burn themselves into your skin upon contact. These jellies are far from common and are easy to spot. Keep an eye out for them as you paddle. If you see one, you will likely see others. Stay out of the water or exercise caution if that's the case. If you plan on snorkeling or diving, it's a good idea to take meat tenderizer along with you to treat any potential jelly stings. Urine is also effective.

Neither sea lice nor man-of-wars are reasons to fear the water. You will know beforehand if they are out there during your trip. Watch where you're going and take precautions; after all, they are less a threat than everyday traffic.

long white ribbon of Boca Chica Beach. Ahead lies nothing but the unseen reef, the Gulf Stream, and Cuba. You will likely find fellow travelers along your route—hawksbill turtles with dark, round eyes, eagle rays lifting their wing tips up with the delicate precision of a ballerina.

Then you'll draw up to the green channel marker at West Washerwoman. The patch reef itself lies just to the west. Be sure to anchor your boat in a sandy section. Never anchor on coral. Moor your boat up to your dive partner's, secure your hatches and paddles, and hoist your dive flag. Take turns exploring the water with your snorkeling partner. Once you've both successfully gotten out of and back into your kayaks, head down under to explore the reef together. This patch reef is more open to the ocean, so it attracts bigger fish and bigger schools than patch reefs closer to shore. You will probably see several sharks here, mostly nurse sharks. Luxuriant purple sea fans and sea plumes sway in the current, a phenomenon unique to reefs in Florida and the Caribbean. Parrotfish abound here, as do angelfish, blue tangs, wrasses, and damselfish. Jellyfish live here, too, and you're most likely to see them after a strong southerly blow. Keep an eye peeled for them as you snorkel, and stay near your partner. A Portuguese man-of-war's sting can be painful, but it can be treated with a sprinkle of meat tenderizer and an aspirin to reduce swelling.

With all this water around you, don't forget to drink plenty of fresh water every hour. There are so many amazing diversions that it's sometimes hard to remember there's a tropical sun beating down on you. Give yourself plenty of time in the water but also enough time for a leisurely paddle back. Just like a day at the beach, a day snorkeling can tire you out.

When you're ready to head back to the launch site, take a long look at the shoreline. You'll see a slight swelling in Saddlehill Key's green profile on your left and a sliver of white farther west along Boca Chica Key. Head for Saddlehill, adjusting your course as you get closer in. Shark Key Channel is well marked, and houses along Geiger Key's eastern shore help to distinguish that particular piece of green land from the many others in the blue waters of the Lower Keys.

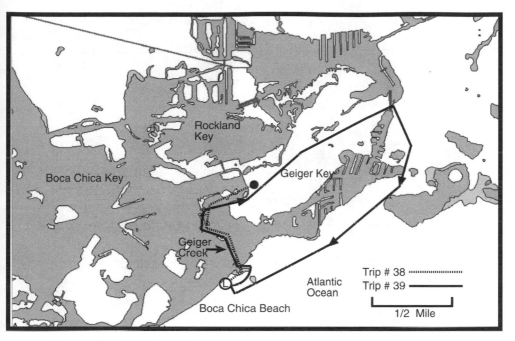

3.16. Geiger Creek: Trips # 38–39

Trip # 38

Geiger Creek

Launch Site: MM 10.8 (oceanside) onto Boca Chica Road
Location: Geiger Key
Paddling Time: 1 hour
Comments: Easy paddle through a pretty mangrove creek on the edge of the ocean. Great for kids.
Note: This trip borders on the Boca Chica Naval Air Station. During the winter many training flights are conducted here. They are very loud but fascinating for those interested in aviation.

This short little trip is easy and relaxing for anyone, and kids especially love it. You start on the ocean, but have to paddle only a few minutes along its shoreline before entering the wide mouth of Geiger Creek. Gradually the creek narrows and becomes more tunnel-like as the mangrove branches knit themselves into a dense canopy. As you paddle through these tunnels, you will likely flush great blue herons and other birds from their roosts, often following them down the creek for several hundred yards before they lift off through breaks in the canopy. Fish abound here.

To reach the launch site, turn oceanside off U.S. 1 at MM 10.8 onto Boca Chica Road. Follow this road for about three miles, almost to its dead end. Park alongside pretty Boca Chica Beach and portage your gear down to the water's edge. There are some sharp coral outcroppings here, so be careful not to damage your hull. At low tide you may have to pull your boat out to deeper water offshore. This isn't very bothersome, and you'll find plenty of water a few minutes ahead when you enter Geiger Creek.

Head east (left) up the coast of Boca Chica Key for about five minutes until you see a bridge on your left. This is Boca Chica Road. Pass under the bridge and enter the wide mouth of Geiger Creek. Any problems you've had with wind, waves, and tide will stop now that you've entered this protected area. The creek wends its way through open and covered areas, and there are a few little branches that lead off from it.

The paddling here is easy. You might almost feel like you're on an amusement park ride. If the naval air station is conducting flight training, you may even get to see some special effects. Boca Chica Naval Air Station is considered the country's premier air assault training station. Its facilities include flight training systems that were featured in the movie *Top Gun*. Flights are most common during the winter months when bad weather shuts down training at other naval air facilities. Fighter jets with bat wings fly so fast that you often see them without hearing them until several seconds later. Huge transport planes are easy to spot, especially when they disgorge scores of parachuting airmen into the sky. Seeing so many brilliant silk parachutes drifting over your boat is quite a spectacle. They look like jellyfish floating above the ocean.

Geiger Creek makes an abrupt east turn just before it enters a wide interior lagoon. The water in the lagoon is quite shallow, less than one foot at low mean tide, and the area is exposed to winds which can make paddling difficult. But if it's a balmy day with a slight breeze, crossing this lagoon allows you to make a circumnavigation of Geiger Key by way of Similar Sound. This circuit, which takes two and a half hours, is described in trip # 39.

Trip # 39

Circumnavigating Geiger Key

Launch Site: MM 10.8 (oceanside) onto Boca Chica Road
Location: Geiger Key
Paddling Time: 2½ hours
Comments: Mild-weather trip through a mangrove creek, interior lagoon, protected sound, and along the ocean's shore.
Note: This trip borders on the Boca Chica Naval Air Station. During the winter months many training flights are conducted here. They are very loud but fascinating for those interested in aviation. This trip will be more difficult at low tide or if there is a strong wind. Summertime can make the lagoon crossing very hot indeed.

To reach the launch site, turn oceanside off U.S. 1 at MM 10.8 onto Boca Chica Road. Follow this through Geiger Key for three miles until you reach Monroe County–owned Boca Chica Beach. This used to be fringed with swaying palm trees, but these succumbed to lethal yellowing disease several decades ago. A fishing camp and restaurant made it a popular destination for islanders in the 1930s, but the army and later the navy have since occupied the adjacent property. Today, with a new coating of white sand thanks to Hurricane Georges, the beach is popular with sunbathers and beachcombers, but there are no facilities.

On a map it's very hard to tell where Boca Chica Key ends and Geiger Key begins. After completing this trip you'll have a better answer to that question and a better appreciation for the many habitats that comprise the Keys. The trip begins on the ocean, enters a tidal creek, passes through an interior lagoon and then a sound, and emerges by way of a boat channel into the ocean once again. It's a particularly nice trip to take on a cool morning or evening when the wind lies down. Sunrise and sunset not only are beautiful over the ocean, they also give you a chance of seeing more wildlife.

Carefully launch your kayak, mindful of the jagged coral. Then head east (left) up the shoreline until you see the bridge that marks the entrance to Geiger Creek. Here you'll find shade and shelter from the wind. It will take you about a half hour to wind your way through the creek. You're likely to see kingfishers swooping and darting among the mangroves, as well as many herons and egrets. Underwater you'll spot schools of mangrove snappers, jade-colored baitfish, horseshoe crabs, bright orange touch-me-not sponges, and other tidal creek natives. You'll make a sharp right turn when you reach a section of the navy base's road. Here you enter a tiny, canopied mangrove tunnel which spills out into the lagoon that separates Geiger from Boca Chica Key.

Several houses line the south shore of the lagoon, while the navy base occupies the land behind you and to your left. The outlet to the lagoon is due east, but it's probably easier to use the pink house straight ahead in the distance as a reference point. It will take you about half an hour to reach this area. Paddle straight down the length of the lagoon. When you near its eastern shore, keep to the right of the small mangroves that stand in front of the pink house, avoiding both canals that flank the house. Instead continue northeast up the shore past the pink house and the gray one after it. The water will get very skinny as you approach a little jut of land. Here the water will get deeper and you'll see the little creek that flows under the bridge on Boca Chica Road. (You passed over this bridge, just before the turnoff to Tern Road, on your way to the launch site. A green "Geiger Key" sign stands just beyond it.)

You'll probably get curious looks from fishermen casting over your head into Similar Sound from the other side of the bridge—few people make this trip, after all. Head right along the shore, passing between a small mangrove island and the houses that line the sound. Within fifteen minutes you'll be abreast of the end of Geiger Road, marked with a dead-end sign. Bear right here up the channel that passes the public boat ramp and then Geiger Key Marina. This might make a good lunch or dinner spot. They serve beer, soft drinks, and food and host a live band on weekends. (There are also bathrooms here.) This is a popular camping and RV spot, too.

Thread your way through the boat channel and head into the ocean. Bear west, paralleling the shoreline of Geiger Key. You will see the bridge marking the entrance to Geiger Creek. Continue paddling along the ocean until you see the launch site a few minutes west of the bridge. You will also see the white sand of Boca Chica Beach curving toward Key West. The old roadbed of U.S. 1 extends past the dead-end sign at the "end" of Boca Chica Road. It's a popular walk in winter and great for beachcombing, especially for fishing floats. Roseate spoonbills sometimes feed here, and it's a nice, if overgrown, place to stretch your legs after a long paddle.

Trip # 40

Halfmoon Key

Launch Site: MM 10 (bayside) onto Fourth Street, then Avenue F
Location: Halfmoon Key in the backcountry off Shark Key and Big Coppitt Key
Paddling Time: 1 hour
Comments: Sunset viewing from a backcountry spot close to Key West

The launch site for this trip is the Big Coppitt Key public boat ramp. "Coppitt" is a term dating back many centuries to refer to dense wood-

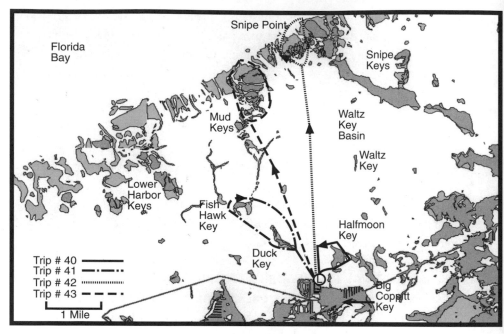

3.17. Big Coppitt Backcountry: Trips # 40–43

lands in England. There are few trees on Big Coppitt today, largely because of hurricane force winds and the lethal yellowing disease that killed most of the coconut palms that used to sway over the island. The Bahamian presence that brought quaint British expressions to the Keys is more visible in Key West's architecture and regional cuisine than it is in the accents of modern-day Big Coppitters. Most people who live here commute to work in nearby Key West, but all of them love the water.

The boat ramp at Big Coppitt is a busy one, and children use it as their swimming hole and playground. To reach it, turn off U.S. 1 at MM 10 at BobaLu's Café and head down Fourth Street for several blocks. Turn left onto Avenue F and follow it, making a right turn onto Barcelona Drive. The boat ramp is at the end of the road, and there is ample parking there.

Launch your kayak and head out the channel. Work your way east (right) for about fifteen minutes, passing the white crosses of Big Coppitt cemetery on your right. Then turn north through the cut that separates this key's peninsula from Halfmoon Key. As you round the eastern shore of Halfmoon Key, the fancy mansions of Shark Key will come into view. Keep heading north and you'll have an even nicer view—the Mud Keys far off toward the Gulf and the massive, mangrovey Snipe Keys sprawling in an eastern arc toward the Overseas Highway.

Nautical charts designate the northern tip of Halfmoon Key as Jim Pent Point. You'll see a large black arrow there, pointing to the interior of the island. A short distance from the sign you'll see two marly promontories with a short dredged canal between them. An old camp used to stand here, and there is an impressive trash pile of rusting cans marking a not-so-ancient midden. Other signs of human habitation are more pleasant, though—a rough-hewn Adirondack-style bench set up on a perfect sunset-watching perch.

You, of course, have an even better seat and a clear view over the backcountry from which to savor the sunset. You'll have enough daylight left once the sun sinks to cross from Halfmoon Key to the Big Coppitt boat ramp, marked by a very tall Chilean pine tree, southeast across the water.

Shark Key is quite an imposing piece of real estate, with its massive iron fence and carefully manicured palms. Back before it was developed, it didn't have such finery, and neither do the keys you'll pass by on this paddle. What they lack in wealthy homes they more than make up for in a wealth of bird life and tranquility. This trip is a good way to unwind from the pressures of work and family. It's also one heck of a nice place to watch the sunset.

Trip # 41

Duck Key and Fish Hawk Key

Launch Site: MM 10 (bayside) onto Fourth Street, then Avenue F
Location: Duck and Fish Hawk Keys, in the backcountry off Big Coppitt Key
Paddling Time: 3 hours
Comments: Bird-watchers' trip to three small backcountry islands near Key West.

To reach the launch site for this trip, turn bayside off U.S. 1 at MM 10, heading past BobaLu's Café on Fourth Street. Take a left turn onto Avenue F, then bear right onto Barcelona Drive. This will lead you to the Big Coppitt public boat ramp. There is plenty of parking there. Launch your boat and head out the canal.

The first of the two Duck Key islands is directly north in front of you. This is a loop trip, so you can let wind, water, and whim inform your choice of which side of the islands to head up. Shallows surround each of the two Duck Keys, making for some interesting underwater views. On one trip I noticed a huge shadow passing next to my kayak—a four-to-five-foot hammerhead shark. Beautiful. Sinister. Big. In my backyard (and his). On another trip a friend and I sat with charts spread out on our laps, studying our course. A houndfish broke the surface of the water dead ahead. It skittered on its backfin across the water toward the Harbor Keys. Just then another houndfish broke the surface right behind it. Then another. Then the water exploded all around us and we were surrounded by a circle of jumping houndfish. We were the ringmasters of an absurd water circus, and we laughed long and loud.

Sharks are common visitors to this area. It's not unusual to see three or four reef sharks at a time here, particularly during the winter. The shallow water here is warm, and sharks like that. It's fascinating to watch their deep gray bodies slice through the water above the mottled brown of the hardbottom seafloor.

This trip doesn't look as impressive as some of the others described in this book, but it offers exceptional chances to view nesting ospreys and other bird life, especially in early spring. Although your motorless kayak makes you less likely to flush birds from their nests than other boaters, take care not to get too close to these birds, their clutches of eggs, and their young. Their absence from their nests for even a few moments exposes their young to the full force of the tropical sun. Bring binoculars to enjoy the view of these fish hawks and their neighbors.

7. Tidal creek near Fish Hawk Key

Birds are the main attraction on Fish Hawk Key, a half-hour paddle north of the second Duck Key. As its name implies, this is prime habitat for ospreys. These are large birds with wingspans up to six feet. Their backs are dark brown or black, and their breasts are entirely white. Ospreys' diet is almost completely composed of fish, and they are magnificent hunters. Take time to watch them hover fifty feet, or even fifty yards, above the water's surface. Once they've spotted their prey, they dive down with such speed that they can break their wings in the process. Ospreys build their nests among the mangroves, sometimes only inches from the water. These nests are sprawling, silvery works of art, added to year after year by pairs of ospreys who mate for life. The young hatch in early spring after a monthlong incubation. In two more months they are able to fly.

There are several osprey nests on Fish Hawk Key and many more throughout the backcountry. Most are so well built that they've survived hurricanes and strong winter storms that have stripped beaches, flung houseboats onto dry land, and wrecked houses built by man. Maybe we can learn something about architecture and engineering from studying them. George de Mestral used the insights he gained from closely examining how cockleburs stuck to his pants to create something we now take for granted—the hook-and-loop tape miracle called Velcro. It's a thought worth considering as you loop around the other side of these three islands and head back for the tall Chilean pine tree that marks the entrance to the Big Coppitt boat ramp.

Trip # 42

Tidal Creeks of the Northern Snipe Keys and Snipe Point Beach

Launch Site: MM 10 (bayside) onto Fourth Street, then Avenue F
Location: Northern Snipe Keys, past Outer Narrows in the backcountry off Big Coppitt Key
Paddling Time: 5 hours

Comments: Daylong paddle to a maze of tidal creeks on the edge of the Gulf.

Note: This is a long trip, so take a partner along for companionship and safety, plus at least a gallon of drinking water per person for hydration, and a nautical chart, compass, rope, and two pocket flares for peace of mind. Try to time your trip so that you'll arrive at Snipe Point after low tide. That way you will avoid the strong tidal surges that affect the area and have plenty of white sand to enjoy. Your route crosses Waltz Key Basin. There is no shelter along most of the route. Don't take this trip if small craft warnings are posted. If thunderstorms, lightning, or waterspouts threaten, head for shore immediately.

To reach the launch site, turn bayside off U.S. 1 at MM 10 and head past BobaLu's Café on Fourth Street. Take a left on Avenue F and then a right onto Barcelona Drive. Park at the Big Coppitt public boat ramp at the end of the drive. Launch your boat and head out the canal. Pause a minute when you reach the entrance to Waltz Key Basin to check for any signs of inclement weather. Ahead of you, about fifteen minutes' paddle

This can be a tricky trip to make. In the winter the UV quotient is lower and the sun merciful, but the prevailing northerlies can blow in excess of fifteen knots, churning up Waltz Key Basin. In the summer the winds lie down, the sun becomes equatorial, and there's a strong possibility of thunderstorms. The threat of lightning strikes and waterspouts is real. Then there's the "people problem"—the boaters who for years have flocked to the white sand beach at Snipe Point. Because beaches, especially secluded beaches, are so rare in the Keys, the area is still quite popular with powerboaters who anchor just offshore, by inches in some cases. Try not to get fixated on the beach at Snipe Point as a destination. If you're lucky enough to have the place to yourself, bask in the glory of its nearshore waters. But go expecting to share the area, and don't be disappointed if a boatful of partygoers has cranked up a stereo and set out lawn chairs. The tidal creeks that crisscross these islands are a kayaker's dream. And if you wait long enough, the powerboaters might leave.

away, is Duck Key (actually two small islands). On the far edge of the horizon to Duck Key's left (west) are the Lower Harbor Keys. Behind Duck Key are the Mud Keys, and across a wide channel from them on the right (east) are the most northerly of the Snipe Keys. Set your course for the point of land just to the right of the channel separating the Mud Keys from the Snipes. If all this sounds confusing now, it will soon sort itself out when the massive length of the lower Snipe Keys comes into view and you can trace their arc out to the edge of the Gulf.

First head for Duck Key, staying on its eastern (right) side. Trip # 41 describes this beautiful area in more detail. Rather than following its shoreline, strike out to the northeast directly across Waltz Key Basin. You will paddle on a course midway between Fish Hawk Key on your left (west) and Waltz Key on your right (east).

It is unbelievably quiet, even lonely, out here. On my last trip across the basin I saw only one boat in more than an hour—a sponging vessel puttering across the basin, one man on the bow eyeing the water. Sponge harvesting has not been regulated since the various marine sanctuaries protecting the Keys were established. Historically, sponging was a chief source of revenue for Bahamians and Cubans. Old-timers used to spread shark oil on the water's surface to calm it before viewing the hardbottom seafloor with a pail fitted with a glass bottom. This primitive magnifying glass allowed them to see the sponges more clearly as they tore them from the seafloor with a three-foot iron prong. Dead sponges were kept in a crawl underneath the boat's deck for a week. Then they were beaten with a wooden bat, scraped with a sharp knife, and soaked and squeezed to remove all animal matter and sand. The clean sponges were then hung to dry. Today the industry is coming under close scrutiny as scientists cite studies that show the importance of sponges in filtering seawater and providing habitat for juvenile fish and worms. Spongers also are suspected of contributing to water pollution by dumping the by-products (dead organisms) of cleaning and drying sponges directly overboard. Restrictions or a total ban on sponging are being considered as a means of insuring a healthy marine habitat.

As you paddle on past Waltz Key, remember to drink plenty of fresh water and reapply sunscreen. You are almost halfway to Snipe Point, and you will have been gone a little over an hour. Another hour and a quarter will take you past Outer Narrows to the southern edge of the maze of islands you've spent so long paddling toward. As you approach them, note the speed and direction of tidal flow between Waltz Key Basin and the Gulf of Mexico. The tide can be overpowering here. If it is strong, head east, staying in the lee of the three northern island clusters that make up this portion of the Snipe Keys. Tie up to stout mangrove branches and wait for the tide to subside.

When you continue making your way around the western corner of the Snipes, you'll get your reward. Cormorants roost on the mangroves here. I've seen more than forty at a time bending the boughs. Zillions of baitfish pulse through the nearshore waters, and the view out to the Gulf is magical. The whole area hums with life. It is riddled with mangrove tidal creeks perfect for kayaking and closed to powerboaters. But if Snipe Point is on your agenda, I'd suggest going there first. Winding through the mangroves can be disorienting, and it's best to get the lay of the land.

Head right (east, then northeast) along the Gulf-side shores of these tiny islands for Snipe Point. The beach here is unmistakable and very welcome. Not only is the view paradisical but the water here is the perfect depth for swimming and snorkeling. If you visit the point after a spring rain, you're also likely to be greeted by a most unexpected sight. Here in the tropics on a tiny wild beach is a prickly pear cactus, and if your timing is right it will be covered with waxy, translucent yellow blossoms.

You can retrace your route back to the maze of tidal creeks or venture through one of the many cuts that slice through these islets. Consulting a chart and compass can help you to orient yourself. If you lose your bearings, don't worry. If you've gone too far into the Gulf, you'll know it— every speck of land will be to your south. All you'll need to do is turn around and head the other way.

Which is what you'll do on the return leg of your trip. Retrace your route past Outer Narrows and into Waltz Key Basin. Keep midway between Waltz Key on your left (east) and Fish Hawk Key on your right (west). Stay on the east side of Duck Key, and look for the tall Chilean pine that marks the Big Coppitt boat ramp.

Trip # 43

Mud Keys

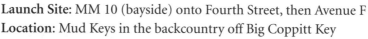

Launch Site: MM 10 (bayside) onto Fourth Street, then Avenue F
Location: Mud Keys in the backcountry off Big Coppitt Key
Paddling Time: 5 to 6 hours
Comments: Daylong paddle to a group of backcountry islands with beautiful vistas, great snorkeling, and a beach.
Note: This is a long trip, so take along a partner for companionship and safety, plus at least a gallon of water per person for hydration, and a nautical chart, compass, rope, and two pocket flares for peace of mind. Your route crosses Waltz Key Basin. There is no shelter along most of the route. Don't take this trip if small-craft warnings are posted. If thunderstorms, lightning, or waterspouts threaten, head for shore immediately. Try to time your trip so that you'll arrive just after low tide. That way you will avoid the strong tidal surges that affect this area and you'll have plenty of "instant beaches." Beaches are rare in the Florida Keys, and secluded ones are particularly coveted. Take this trip on a weekday if possible, and not during spring break. Be prepared to find "your" beach already occupied by powerboats or commercial kayak group tour boats.

The Muds are a popular destination for powerboats, sailboats, and commercial kayak tours (which bring a dozen or more kayakers out to the area by houseboat). Prepare to share. The western and southern areas of the Muds are usually the least crowded and the most suitable for kayakers. If you time your trip to arrive at low tide, you will find many "instant beaches" unreachable by deeper-drafted boats.

To reach the launch site, turn off U.S. 1 at MM 10 and head past BobaLu's Café on Fourth Street. Take a left on Avenue F and then a right onto Barcelona Drive. Park at the Big Coppitt public boat ramp at the end of the drive. Launch your boat and head out the canal. When you reach the entrance to Waltz Key Basin, take a minute to check the weather conditions. An incoming tide or strong north wind can make paddling here

Like the brightly painted Russian dolls that nest one inside the other, the Mud Keys fit together smallest to largest. Their southern and western shores hold tiny islets and small tidal passages that make for premier kayaking. Along the northern shore are mangrove tunnels and tidal creeks. The many sandbars and shoals that ring these islands provide plenty of chances for viewing wading birds and for creating "instant beaches" perfect for a few shallow-draft kayaks. And the water here on the edge of the Gulf of Mexico can be the most beautiful anywhere in the Keys, ranging from turquoise to aqua to pale robin's egg blue. Superior water clarity and underwater visibility make it almost mandatory to snorkel here.

tough going. Look at your chart and compare it with the landscape spread before you. Ahead of you lies Duck Key and beyond it on the far horizon are the Mud Keys. They are flanked by wide channels on either side. The Lower Harbor Keys are to their west (left); the Snipe Keys are to their east (right). You may even be able to see the Bay Keys far off to your left, opposite Key West.

Set your course for the small key at the far right of the sprawling Mud Key chain. You will paddle along the eastern shore of the Muds, arriving between the two northernmost islands. This will let you see who, if anyone, is enjoying the beach before you explore other parts of the island chain. You can then work your way north to the edge of the Gulf or down the interesting western shore of these keys. If you prefer exploring a small tidal creek first, head up along the eastern shore of the northernmost key almost to the edge of the Gulf. You'll find the mouth of the creek there.

To begin your journey, paddle first for fifteen minutes to the southeastern (right) edge of small Duck Key, directly in front of you. Then head out across Waltz Key Basin on a course for the small key on the right of the Mud Key group. You'll have few reference points along the way other than Fish Hawk Key to your left (west). If you'd like to take a break en route to the Muds, this is a good spot, albeit one that will add about a half hour to your paddling time. A trip to Duck and Fish Hawk Keys is described in trip #41.

Drink fresh water at least every half hour, even if you're not thirsty. This is a long paddle.

After two hours of steady paddling you'll reach the southernmost of the Mud Keys. From here it's another fifteen-minute paddle to the main channel that separates the two largest islands in the group. Entering this channel, you'll find herons and egrets enjoying the quiet of their back-country home. At the western end of the channel lies a sandy beach. If you're lucky, it will be yours alone to enjoy.

If you've got plenty of time and would like to explore the Gulf side of the Muds, head north. You can paddle along the inlets that dot this shore-line before looping south down the keys' eastern shore. Near the top of the northernmost key you'll find a pretty tidal creek.

The southwestern shore of the Muds holds the most interest for kayak-ers. There are many small islets, quiet lagoons, sandy shoals, and tidal passages. By working your way south down this shore, you'll be able to make your tour of the Muds a loop trip filled with adventure but no risk of becoming disoriented. The water here is shallower and more protected that elsewhere in the Muds, making it a perfect spot for snorkeling and swimming. Schools of green gobies and brilliant silversides provide fan-tastic visual images underwater. Water clarity and visibility here are re-markable.

After a pleasant day in these beautiful waters, give yourself plenty of time for the two hours of paddling it will take you to return to Big Cop-pitt Key. By now your muscles may be tired, and you may have that lazy feeling that a day in the sun brings. Stop en route at Fish Hawk Key if you wish, particularly if you like bird-watching. As you paddle south toward Duck Key, keep an eye out for the distinctive tall green Chilean pine tree that marks the entrance to the Big Coppitt boat ramp.

If you're hungry, once you've loaded your gear onto your car, try the home cooking, great pizzas, and plentiful vegetables at BobaLu's South-ern Café before hitting U.S. 1.

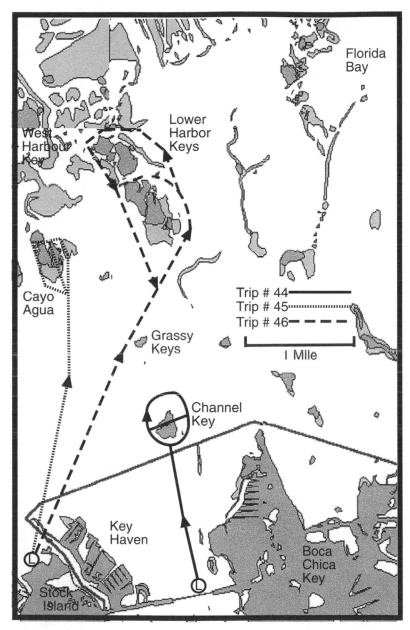

Florida
Bay

Lower
Harbor
Keys

West
Harbour
Key

Cayo
Agua

Trip # 44
Trip # 45
Trip # 46

I Mile

Grassy
Keys

Channel
Key

Key
Haven

Boca
Chica
Key

Stock
Island

3.18. Channel Key, Cayo Agua, and Lower Harbor Keys: Trips # 44–46

Trip # 44

Channel Key

Launch Site: MM 6 (bayside)
Location: Channel Key in the backcountry just north of Boca Chica Channel
Paddling Time: 1½ hours
Comments: Short trip to a mangrove island cut in half by a little-used boat channel. A nice place to watch the sunset near Key West.
Note: Because ospreys nest at the eastern entrance of the channel, the U.S. Fish and Wildlife Service may close access to this channel in the spring.

This is certainly not an exotic put-in site. The Keys' only highway carries a nonstop stream of cars behind it. A busy boat channel spews every kind of boat and ski underneath the highway and into the broad V of Boca Chica Channel. And dead ahead, stretching out just in front of your destination, lie massive power lines humming with electricity.

Never mind all that. In half an hour you can paddle out to Channel Key and start living by the local saying "Paradise begins a quarter mile offshore."

To reach the launch site, pull onto the wide gravel shoulder on the bayside of U.S. 1 at MM 6, on the west side of Boca Chica Channel. You can easily launch here. As you look out into the backcountry, you'll see three keys facing you. Channel Key is the one on the left, the only one that lies completely beyond the power lines.

With an eye out for speedboats cutting through Boca Chica Channel, paddle straight out. The relatively deep water here makes this a good choice for a sunset paddle. Knowing that you won't run into any skinny water on the way back and that the lights of U.S. 1 will guide you home, you can relax and enjoy the view.

Within a half hour you'll reach the southern shore of Channel Key. The great green grass beds here are dense and healthy. Work your way up the island's west coast for a view of the Harbor Keys, then double back and enter the dredged waterway that splits Channel Key in half horizontally (west to east). After your paddle across open water, it will probably feel good to be in this intimate, winding space. Schools of baitfish cloud the water, which can be exceptionally clear for a place so near to civilization. You will likely see ospreys here and their huge silvery nests as well. Frigate birds also frequent the key, flying impossibly high in the cobalt sky.

If you're here at sunset, you'll be treated to a vision of the sun's warm rays of light illuminating the mangroves' prop roots. Turn to face the sun's last rays before paddling back toward the bridge. As the light fades, you'll see car lights streaming red and white along the highway and the gas station's marquee lit up. By the time darkness falls, you'll be loading up your kayak, and then your lights will join the others streaming down the highway.

Trip # 45

Around and through Cayo Agua

Launch Site: MM 4.1 (bayside) onto College Road, then to Florida Keys Community College
Location: Cayo Agua, in the backcountry off Stock Island
Paddling Time: 3 hours
Comments: Dense cluster of keys separated by both wide and small channels. Near Key West.

If you have your own kayak and you're near Key West, this is a nice place to spend a morning or afternoon. By venturing into the backcountry instead of the more popular snorkel, dive, and fishing spots "out front" in the Atlantic, you'll avoid the crowds and get a real taste of what makes the Keys different from the rest of South Florida.

To reach the launch site, turn bayside at the stoplight at MM 4.1 near the Key West golf course. Head down College Drive past "Mount Trashmore," where Key Westers' compacted garbage reaches for the sky. Turn left at Florida Keys Community College and bear to the right around the marine propulsion lab and the swimming pool. Park behind the Public Safety Building. At the far northern end of the lot you can go down an embankment of coral rock. You can launch your kayak here in between the mangroves.

As you look out over the waters of the Great White Heron National Wildlife Refuge, you'll see three of the Bay Keys off to your left. Another small island lies just to the west of the mass of Cayo Agua, which looms on the horizon past the power lines offshore.

Begin by paddling under the power pole that most closely resembles a ladder, setting your course directly for Cayo Agua. Jet Skis sometimes zip through the nearshore waters here, but they are prohibited in the refuge waters that lie less than half an hour's paddle away. The seafloor here is mostly hardbottom—full of large loggerhead and vase sponges, a playground for rays, turtles, and sharks.

After an hour of paddling, the emerging shoreline of Cayo Agua will become clearer. To find the tidal creeks that riddle this key, head for the tallest vegetation in the middle of the shoreline. The widest of these channels holds lovely mangroves, tall and stout. At low tide, white salt marks are visible for half a foot above the water line, indicating the intensity with which water can stream through this isolated area. Undulating beds of seagrass cover the bottoms of the main channel and of the tidal creeks separating different portions of this densely packed island group. On a still day you'll think you're peering into an aquarium stocked full of mangrove snappers, bonefish, gobies, silversides, fire sponges, and toothy barracudas.

By circumnavigating the key you can enjoy views of the Lower Harbor Keys (described in trip # 46) across shallow water to the east. Coming along the western edge of the island, you'll see Boca Chica and the Bay

Keys. There are many small creeks to explore en route, allowing you to take in the bird life and other wonders of this quiet spot at the edge of the Great White Heron National Wildlife Refuge. It is especially lovely and vibrant at low tide, when sandbars dot the extremely shallow waters on the western edge of the key.

When you turn for home, look for Mount Trashmore, highest spot in the Keys, and the blue and white buildings of Florida Keys Community College near it. You will recognize the Public Safety Building, behind which you parked, as you draw closer to Stock Island.

Trip # 46

Lower Harbor Keys

Launch Site: MM 4.1 (bayside) onto College Drive, then to Florida Keys Community College
Location: Lower Harbor Keys in the backcountry off Boca Chica Key
Paddling Time: 4 to 5 hours
Comments: Daylong trip to an island group poised on the Gulf not far from Key West.
Note: Although a bit shorter than a trip to the northern Snipe Keys or Mud Keys, this is still a long trip. Take along a partner for companionship and safety, plus at least a gallon of water per person for hydration, and a nautical chart, compass, rope, and two pocket flares for peace of mind. There is no shelter along most of the route. Don't take this trip if small-craft warnings are posted. If thunderstorms, lightning, or waterspouts threaten, head for shore immediately. Watch for strong tidal currents in the Lower Harbor Keys. Try to plan your trip so that you'll arrive just after low tide—that way you'll avoid the strong tidal surges that affect this area and you'll be able to enjoy many beautiful sandbars.

Ah, the Harbor Keys! They're my favorites. They're close to Key West, yet feel very remote, poised on the edge of the Gulf of Mexico. The islands are separated by tidal creeks and sandbars that provide interesting kayaking and nice resting places. Because there is no beach and (despite their name) no real harbor, powerboaters and commercial outfitters tend to stay away. And most important of all, they lie on some of the most beautiful aquamarine water in the entire Florida Keys.

The best launch site for this trip is behind the parking lot of Florida Keys Community College. To reach it, turn bayside at the stoplight onto College Drive at MM 4.1. Head down the road past the waste management collection site known locally as Mount Trashmore, past a school, and into the community college opposite the hospital. Bear right around the marine propulsion lab, then past the swimming pool, to the parking lot behind the Public Safety Building. At the far northern end of the parking lot you can descend a bank of coral rock and launch from a clear spot among the mangroves.

From your vantage point here at the water's edge you can see three islands that make up the Bay Keys on your left. Parallel to the southeasternmost Bay Key is Cayo Agua, which is described in trip # 45. The Lower Harbor Keys begin east of Cayo Agua, spreading in a northwestern arc across shallow water that empties into the Gulf of Mexico. Head for the island east of Cayo Agua. Once there, you can paddle up one side of the Lower Harbors and down the other or loop in and out of the many tidal passages.

The trip through these waters is usually a solitary one. There is little boat traffic once you have passed under the cable lines that parallel U.S. 1 and entered the Great White Heron National Wildlife Refuge. Sharks and rays love to race across these flats, and you will probably see sea turtles as well. Hardbottom communities of sponges give the seafloor a desertlike look in places, while thick meadows of seagrass sway in others. After paddling for about an hour you'll reach some shallow grass beds between Cayo Agua on your left (west) and the Grassy Keys on your right (east). In another half hour you'll reach the southernmost of the Lower Harbor Keys. A welcoming committee of cormorants, ibis, pelicans, herons, and nesting ospreys will noisily herald your approach. If you've timed your trip to arrive at low tide, you'll look up to a Caribbean vista of magnificent white sandbars dotting the aqua and turquoise water. Work your way northeast up the indented shore of each of the keys, exploring the creeks and inlets that abound there. Farther north lies a lagoon that's a perfect lunch spot, and a cluster of several small islands. Here you can watch a bird's flight in its entirety, uninterrupted by buildings or noise or any obstacle whatsoever, from its first lifting movements to its final coming to rest. This can make you feel more relaxed, more attentive, more a part of the living, breathing world.

You may want to continue your trip northwest to West Harbor Key. It has a beautiful view of the Gulf and some very good fishing. Be aware that falling and rising tides in this area are quite strong, especially in the deeper channels. Wait in the safety of some mangroves for the tidal current to subside or you risk being swept into the Gulf. As a kayaker you will probably have more fun exploring the ins and outs of the Lower Harbor Keys than paddling to West Harbor Key. To avoid getting lost here pencil in your route on a photocopied chart or temporarily tie bright strips of cloth on mangroves where you turn, then retrace your route.

When you're ready to head back to the launch site, work your way down either side of the island chain. You will see a slight bulge in the shoreline ahead of you marking the impressive mound of compacted garbage at Mount Trashmore. Set your sights on this, correcting your route east of it as the blue and white buildings of the community college come into focus. It will take you about an hour and a half to reach the parking lot behind the white Public Safety Building where you launched your boat.

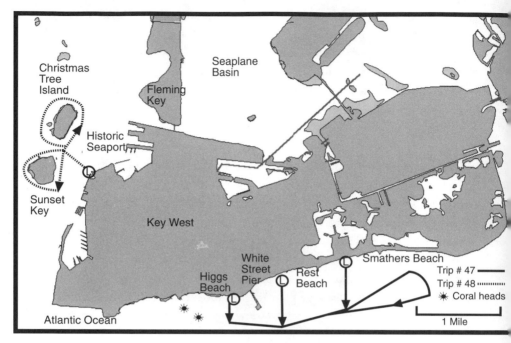

3.19. Key West: Trips # 47–48

Trip # 47

Key West Beaches and Coral Heads

Launch Site: MM 1 (Truman Avenue) onto A1A, then Atlantic Boulevard
Location: Higgs Beach to Smathers Beach and South Beach, Key West
Paddling Time: 1½ hours
Comments: Easy paddle along Key West's most popular beaches to a small patch reef very near shore.
Note: Kayak rentals are available at Higgs Beach and Smathers Beach. If you have two cars, you can also do this as a shuttle trip by parking one car at Smathers Beach and the other at Higgs Beach. If you plan on snorkeling the coral heads of the patch reef, bring a snorkeling partner, an anchor,

a dive flag, and a length of strong rope. Be very careful to anchor in a sandy patch of seafloor. Never anchor on coral. Practice getting out of and back into your kayak in deep water before you take this trip. You will be anchoring in water that is from seven to thirteen feet deep. Don't take the snorkeling portion of this trip if you are not confident of your swimming or snorkeling ability or your ability to pull yourself into your kayak from deep water.

People come to Key West for lots of reasons—because it's the end of the road (home of the self-proclaimed Southernmost Point in the United States), because it has a long history of fun-loving, larger-than-life characters (Ernest Hemingway, Tennessee Williams, Mel Fisher, and Jimmy Buffett), because of the architecture (a fascinating mix of Bahamian, New England colonial, Spanish, and modern), because of the weather (100 percent frost-free). And, ironically, because of the beaches. Visions of white sand beaches, including our famous clothing-optional one, seem to be a part of every tourist's mental image of Key West. Yet much of the sand on Key West's beaches today is imported by the boatful from the Bahamas.

The beaches begin just past Cow Key Channel, which separates Key West from neighboring Stock Island. As it spreads past the old fort of East Martello Tower and then the airport, the beach widens. This stretch of groomed white sand, dotted with food vendors, a boat launch, and bathing and bathroom facilities, is known as Smathers Beach. A row of highrise condos built in the real estate boom of the late 1970s separates

---

For most people these beaches are a pleasant place to beachcomb, read a book, work on a tan, or build sand castles. By launching a kayak from them, a paddler can get a different perspective—a panoramic view of Key West's southern shore, including its two historic forts and the islands that lie west of Key West, past the end of the road. Just off South Beach lies an extra bonus for kayakers, a small patch reef that can easily be explored.

Smathers from the next public beach, the recently restored Harvey Rest Beach. On the other side of the White Street Fishing Pier and the adjacent old fort of West Martello Tower lies the beach most frequented by locals, Higgs Beach. Here is another bathhouse, picnic shelters, a playground, seaside restaurant, and kayak rental stand. Just past Higgs Beach lies the historic Casa Marina hotel with its own very posh palm-fringed private beach, then tiny Dog Beach, and clothing-optional South Beach. At the southwestern tip of the island lies the beautiful, if perennially rocky, beach at Fort Zachary Taylor State Park.

To reach the launch site, head for Key West's southern shore by turning left onto A1A at the split just west of Cow Key Channel. This will take you along the Atlantic Ocean, past the airport and then to Smathers Beach. The road jogs to the right onto Bertha (First) Street. Follow this for one

A Bittersweet Monument

The sugar sands of Higgs Beach cloak a tragedy that occurred 140 years ago. In 1860 the U.S. Navy interdicted three American-owned slave ships off Key West en route to Havana. Although the ships' captains offered substantial bribes to the officers who boarded their vessels, naval officials brought 1,432 African men, women, and children safely ashore to freedom. The three thousand residents of Key West joined the U.S. Marshall in providing the Africans with food, clothing, and medicine. More than eleven hundred of the castaways were eventually repatriated to Africa, settling in Liberia with the aid of the American Colonization Society. They included a baby born in Key West. But the inhuman, unsanitary conditions of the Middle Passage claimed the lives of 294 men, women, and children. A Key West carpenter built wooden coffins for the dead, who were buried beneath the coral sand on Higgs Beach. Few people know of this sad episode in Keys history, but local citizens' efforts led in 2001 to the erection of a memorial plaque. A museum is being planned to honor the survivors and those who perished.

block before turning left onto Atlantic Avenue. Once past the condos, you'll see Harvey Rest Beach, then the White Street Pier. Turn left into the parking lot of Higgs Beach, just past West Martello Tower. You can launch your kayak from anywhere along the beach.

Launching from Higgs Beach and heading out to sea, you'll encounter another chapter in Key West history. You'll paddle first past West Martello Tower. Like its twin up the shoreline, this tower was built between 1862 and 1864 as part of a Civil War defense system anchored by Fort Zachary Taylor at the island's southwestern tip. The tower's architecture and name were based on a defensive model devised by ancient Corsican military strategists. Neither East nor West Martello Tower was ever completed, and no cannons were ever hoisted onto their battlements. In fact, West Martello became a target for soldiers at Fort Taylor and a source of "borrowed" bricks for many Key West gardens. Appropriately, it's now the home of the Key West Garden Society, and well worth a visit. The vegetation in Key West is much lusher than elsewhere in the Keys, but this is a result of human habitation, not geology or botany. The water from rooftops and cisterns, the soil built up through more than a century and a half's accumulated composting, and the careful planting and cultivation of gardens and trees give the island a verdant Caribbean look. Despite the loss of 25 percent of the island's trees in Hurricane Georges, its gardens are still impressive.

Less impressive, to be sure, is the low-lying mangrove jumble lying midway between one massive block of oceanfront condos and the next as you paddle past the White Street Fishing Pier and head east up the key. This is the Berg property, recently acquired by the city of Key West. Once a highly coveted piece of real estate, it became a derelict spot filled with trash when legal brakes were applied to the development juggernaut. It has recently been cleaned up so that it can prove its real worth by insuring a bit of drainage for this built-up part of the island. A mangrove swamp stood here until the 1950s, and water flowed freely through it. Now this ragged bit of shoreline and the salt ponds of the island's interior are all that's left of that ecosystem.

Smathers Beach lies less than half an hour's paddle from Higgs Beach. It is usually crowded with sun worshippers, windsurfers, and sunfish sailors. If you like a beach scene, this is it. There are food booths, umbrella and chair rentals, and a nice bathhouse and water fountain. Fifteen minutes farther up the key is the East Martello Tower. Its architecture is more intact than West Martello's and it serves as a museum operated by the Key West Art and Historical Society. Its galleries depict Key West's maritime history and include permanent exhibits of works by acclaimed folk artists Mario Sanchez and Stanley Papio.

Forty years ago, when tensions mounted between the United States and Cuba, all of Key West's southern beaches from Smathers to Trumbo Point next to Fort Zachary Taylor bristled with missiles aimed across the Florida Straits. Today the trade embargo against Cuba is loosening, and there is quiet talk in city and county offices about how Key West will handle relations with Cuba once the ban on American tourists visiting that island is abolished. It's a conundrum worth puzzling over as you paddle west back down the key toward Higgs Beach.

Don't forget to enjoy the view out to sea and under the water, too. Fish thrive in these nearshore waters, and water clarity off Key West has improved dramatically since citizens approved a $23-million public works bond to overhaul the island's sewage and drainage systems.

In 2001 a protected swim area was set aside on the south side of the island from South Beach (off Duval Street) to White Street Pier. When complete it will encompass waters two hundred yards out into the ocean, prohibit motorized watercraft of any kind except in two beach access channels, and establish a no-take zone for fishing. Swimmers and snorkelers will appreciate the safety this area provides, and marine species will appreciate the new coral substrate being created here.

You can explore the coral heads in this area by paddling west past the boat channel opposite the Wyndham Casa Marina Resort. The coral heads lie in seven feet of water directly off South Beach, next to Atlantic Shores resort. Be sure to raise a dive flag, moor your boats together, secure your hatches and paddles, and anchor up securely in a sandy spot before exploring this area underwater. Never anchor on coral. Take turns with your snorkeling partner, swimming or snorkeling one at a time so that someone is in a boat if the other needs assistance. Take turns getting back into your boat before both of you snorkel the patch reef together. You'll see tiny brilliantly colored tropical fish here, as well as toothy barracudas, angelfish, parrotfish, sea fans, and brain coral. By venturing a few hundred feet offshore you'll see a whole other side of Key West.

Conchs

The word "Conch" seems omnipresent in Key West. Local high school athletes go by the name Fighting Conchs. The high school dance team is known as the Conchettes. There are Conch restaurants, Conch liquor stores, Conch dry cleaners. The motorized tram that carries sightseeing tourists around town is called the Conch Train.

Marine biologists identify conchs (pronounced "konks") as members of the class Gastropoda. Humans have eaten their snail-like flesh for centuries, and conch fritters have become the definitive dish of both the Keys and the Bahamas. For centuries sailors have blown melodies using pink and beige conch shells. Each year in March there is a conch blowing contest, with several age divisions, held in Key West.

"Conch" is also the nickname for native-born residents of the Keys, especially those of Bahamian and British descent. Conchs live in Conch houses, usually white clapboard ones whose porch ceilings are painted sky blue in homage to the sea. Conchs speak with a distinct Brooklynesque accent peppered with colloquialisms. Conchs call one another "Bubba," and are a generous, genial community well worth getting to know. Newcomers to the area, when properly acculturated, become "freshwater Conchs."

Trip # 48

Just West of Key West

Launch Site: Simonton Street Boat Launch
Location: Key West
Paddling Time: 1½ hours
Comments: Easy paddle around two small islands with unique views of Key West's historic Mallory Square and seaport.
Note: Crossing the ship channel can be tricky, especially at sunset when

Key West is the end of the road for travelers who've come by car. But just one block from busy, flamboyant Duval Street, the end-all and be-all of many tourists' pilgrimage, lies a launch site that will give you a different adventure altogether. By paddling less than a mile offshore you can see where two of the city's many subcultures make their homes—the live-aboard boaters of Christmas Tree Island and the superrich of Sunset Key.

many charter boats churn up the water. Early morning and afternoon are less crowded.

Look at a nautical chart of Key West's environs and you won't see either of these keys listed. Instead they'll be called Wisteria Island and Tank Island, respectively. Locals unanimously refer to Wisteria as Christmas Tree Island, for reasons now unclear, and quite a few locals live on sailboats tucked along its northern shore. Sunset Key is a newer name, one proffered by developers who thought Tank Island sounded less savory and too military, its recent history as a storage site for navy fuel tanks notwithstanding. Today it glistens like a diamond in a rich sapphire setting, its multi-million-dollar homes just a water taxi ride away from Key West's buskers and chicken-filled alleys.

To reach the launch site, head into Key West along U.S. 1, bearing right at the split on the west end of the Cow Key Channel bridge. This will put you on South Roosevelt Boulevard, now home to a string of shopping centers, once home to low mangroves and shallow water. You'll pass Garrison Bight Marina on your right, home to Key West's Charter Row, then pass Bayview Park on your left with its José Martí Memorial. At this point U.S. 1 takes on a second identity as Truman Avenue. (Several presidents have visited Key West over the years, but Truman's name rings loudest here.) Keep your eyes peeled for Simonton Street, one block east of Duval. Turn right here and follow it to the water. This is the Simonton Street Boat Launch.

From the launch site you can see both Sunset Key on your left and Christmas Tree Island on your right. Keep a sharp eye out for boat traffic as you cross the busy ship channel and head between the two islands. A figure-eight route will allow you to circumnavigate both keys, giving you nice views of the sandbars of the Lakes Passage west of Key West and Calda Bank to its north. Your view east will include the historic Old Town section of the city, including Mallory Square and the tall red-brick Customs House (now the Key West Museum of Art and History). From the eastern shore of Christmas Tree Island you'll see the fishing and pleasure boats of the historic seaport. The long expanse of Fleming Key, where Navy SEALS train, can also be seen from here.

At low tide ribbons of sand emerge from the waters north of Christmas Tree Island from Pearl Bank all the way to Calda Bank. Dolphins are often spotted here. If you have the time and gauge the tides just right, you'll have your own little beachfront property, and dolphins make good neighbors.

Trip # 49

Dry Tortugas National Park: Day Trip

Launch Site: Historic Seaport, Key West (for commercial ferry ride to this island park, 2 hours each way)

Location: Dry Tortugas archipelago, 70 nautical miles west of Key West

Paddling Time: 1 to 3 hours. Because of the remoteness of this area, and the significant cost of getting there, camping overnight and taking several short paddling trips is advised. The trip described here, however, can be taken by visitors who return to Key West the same day.

Comments: Breathtaking paddling through azure waters in a remote area with no services except those provided on the ferry—and the saltwater toilets available on Garden Key. Snorkeling, swimming, beachcombing, and bird-watching are unparalleled in these waters. Historic Fort Jefferson, the largest masonry structure in the Western Hemisphere, provides welcome shade and stunning architecture.

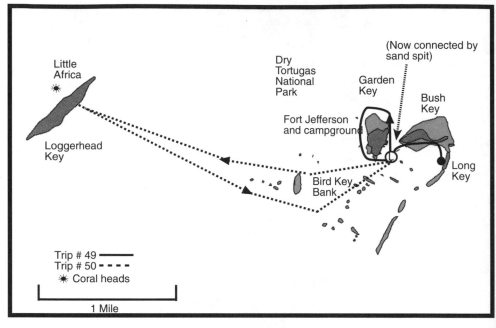

Little
Africa

Loggerhead
Key

Dry
Tortugas
National
Park

Garden
Key

(Now connected by
sand spit)

Bush
Key

Fort Jefferson
and campground

Long
Key

Bird Key
Bank

Trip # 49 ———
Trip # 50 - - - -
✳ Coral heads

1 Mile

3.20. Dry Tortugas National Park: Trips # 49–50

Note: A trip to the Dry Tortugas takes advance planning. This island group is accessible only by ferry from Key West. Two companies currently make the trip daily. (Cost is approximately $95/person plus $35/kayak. Storage space aboard the ferries is limited, and kayak transport must be arranged well in advance. The *Yankee Freedom* cannot take kayaks longer than fifteen feet.) The park, although remote, has become increasingly popular in recent years. Birders flock to the campground on Garden Key in April to observe nesting sooty terns. Boy Scout troops congregate there in June. The vital importance of these remote islands as nesting areas for seabirds and turtles entails severe restrictions on human activities: Loggerhead Key is open to the public only during daylight hours. Bush Key is closed from February through September, and Hospital and Long Keys are both closed year-round. Accepting these restrictions is a small price to pay for ensuring the continued health of these islands. (And as a kayaker you'll want to be on—and in—the water most of the time anyway).

1832. Masked boobies, brown noddies, and magnificent frigate birds nest here as well. The protection of this important rookery led to the area's designation as a wildlife refuge in 1908.

Fort Jefferson's imposing architecture and historical significance led to its preservation as a national monument in 1935. The red brick structure takes up almost the entire landmass of Garden Key, soaring fifty feet into the air, with eight-foot-thick walls and a wraparound moat. Strolling beneath the red brick arches of the three-story fort provides welcome shade from the searing tropical sun and a visual delight as well. Inside the circular fort's protective walls grow verdant ferns, coconut and date palms, orange-flowered geiger trees, night-blooming cereus cacti, and red-fruited ochrosia. The gorgeous 360-degree view from atop the fort's ramparts is like nothing else in the United States.

The vast majority of the park's one hundred thousand annual visitors arrive on the ferry late in the morning, tour the fort, eat a catered lunch, and while away the afternoon swimming and snorkeling along Garden Key's beach. They depart late in the afternoon, returning to Key West barely in time for its famous sunset. If weather conditions are just right—calm seas, little wind, and no rain on the horizon—you could work in a short kayak paddle around Garden Key and nearby Bush and Long Keys on such a day trip. If you choose to do so, be sure to let your captain know your plans. Take a watch, so that you return in time for your ferry's departure. (Otherwise you'll be stranded with no water, food, or tent.) A brief trip to the park's visitor center will provide you with a free park brochure, with a map marking good snorkeling sites and approximate water depths. Nautical charts of the park's waters are usually available for purchase. The ranger on duty can let you know if a change in the weather is expected, too.

Since the ferries dock on the southeastern side of Garden Key, this will serve as your launch site. Let your ferry's crew help you to unload your kayak and paddle. You can store them on the beach next to the dock as you briefly tour the fort and grab a quick lunch. Then, unless prevailing wind or tides dictate otherwise, head left around the dock toward the sand spit that connects Garden and Bush Keys. Until December 2000, a hundred-yard channel separated these islands. Now only a rope and sign designate the boundary. From October until February visitors are welcome to beachcomb along the pristine beaches here, and dead shells found above the high-water line may be collected (although coral, the building block of these islands, may not). Hermit crabs have a knack for choosing the best shells as shelter, so be sure to give each of your treasures a good shake before hauling it back to the ferry!

Paddling along the southern shore of Bush Key provides an excellent opportunity for bird-watching. Magnificent frigates nest on nearby Long Key, as do noddies, sooty terns, and boobies. Stay outside the buoys and approach slowly.

If you are returning to Key West on the afternoon ferry, you may not have enough time to make a loop trip of Long, Bush, and Garden Keys. Instead, retrace your route across Bush Key's southern shore and back to the launch site. From here continue west past the coaling docks. Far off across Southwest Channel you'll see Loggerhead Key with its tall white lighthouse.

Turn north as the swim beach comes into view, and paddle just outside its buoys. Here you'll find excellent snorkeling areas (marked on the park brochure map). Colorful reef fish abound here, and the water is clearer than anywhere else in the keys.

The red brick seawall of Fort Jefferson provides a perfect backdrop as you continue to paddle north and then east around Garden Key. The view out to sea provides a reference for where you are—only tiny Hospital Key is visible on the horizon; everything else is a changeable, watery blue.

Check your time. You may have to portage your kayak over the sand spit between Garden and Bush Keys so that you don't miss your ferry. If you have extra time, explore the northern shore of Bush Key. Excellent snorkeling spots abound here.

Be sure to arrive at the dock at least twenty minutes early so that the ship's crew can load your kayak back onto the boat. That way you can relax and enjoy one last look at the splendor around you before heading back to Key West.

FYI:

Daily ferry service to Dry Tortugas National Park is available from

Sunny Days Catamarans

1326 10th Street

Key West, FL 33040
(305) 296-5556
and from
The Yankee Fleet
P.O. Box 5903-B
Key West, FL 33045
(305) 294-0939
Additional information on Dry Tortugas National Park is available from
Superintendent
Dry Tortugas National Park
P.O. Box 6208
Key West, FL 33041
www.nps.gov/drto

Trip # 50

Dry Tortugas National Park: Overnight Camp

Launch Site: Historic Seaport, Key West (for commercial ferry ride to this island park, 2 hours each way)
Location: Dry Tortugas archipelago, 70 nautical miles west of Key West
Paddling Time: 3 hours
Comments: Challenging paddle through remote aquamarine waters filled with coral reefs, across a deep channel to a pristine island at the very end of the Keys archipelago.
Note: A trip to the Dry Tortugas takes advance planning. The island group is accessible only by ferry from Key West. Two companies currently make the trip daily. (Cost is approximately $130/person for overnight campers, plus $35/kayak. Storage space aboard the ferries is limited, and kayak transport must be arranged well in advance.) Limited camping (ten sites) is available on a first-come-first-served basis; groups of ten or more must obtain a permit in advance. The park brochure keeps its ad-

vice to campers brief and to the point: "You must provide for your own existence. The park has no housing, water, meals, bathing facilities, or supplies." The park, although remote, has become increasingly popular in recent years. Birders flock to the campground on Garden Key in April to observe nesting sooty terns. Boy Scout troops congregate there in June. The vital importance of these remote islands as nesting areas for seabirds and turtles entails severe restrictions on human activities: Loggerhead Key is open to the public only during daylight hours. Bush Key is closed from February through September, and Hospital and Long Keys are both closed year-round. Accepting these restrictions is a small price to pay for ensuring the continued health of these islands. (And as a kayaker you'll want to be on—and in—the water most of the time anyway).

Paddling to Loggerhead Key requires advanced skill, optimal weather, a life jacket, several flares, and the company of at least one other person. This is a very remote area. If you plan on snorkeling or diving, bring a partner, an anchor, a dive flag, and a length of strong rope. Be very careful to anchor in a sandy patch of seafloor. Never anchor on coral. Practice getting out of and back into your kayak in deep water before you take this trip. Don't take this trip if you are not confident of your paddling, swimming, snorkeling, or diving abilities or your ability to pull yourself into your kayak from deep water. Park rangers monitor VHF 16 for emergencies, but they don't man it twenty-four hours a day, and regular VHF doesn't reach Key West. There is an emergency satellite phone on Garden Key ($10/minute, credit cards accepted).

All of the superlatives used in describing trip # 49 apply to this trip as well. But there is something more to be enjoyed if weather, winds, tides, and fate bless you with the opportunity to explore these waters farther from shore. No two people's trips will be the same, so there is no point in summing up what you'll experience. This description will be bare bones, just enough to whet your appetite, to persuade you to buy the NOAA chart and invite a friend or two to join you in an unforgettable paddle to the western edge of Dry Tortugas National Park.

9. Dry Tortugas National Park

Since you'll be camping out for at least one night, be sure to contact both the park and the ferry that will transport you and your gear well in advance of your planned trip. Keep a close eye on the weather. You can get a weeklong forecast, as well as current conditions, from www.intellicast. com. No matter what your television or computer tells you, be sure to check with a ranger at the visitor center on Garden Key before heading out to Loggerhead Key. Let them know your plans, and get the latest update on tides and winds. There is no substitute for local knowledge, and the rangers are understandably tired of rescuing folks who've bitten off more adventure than they can chew—like the kayaker who decided to paddle solo all the way from Key West!

Launch from the beach next to the ferry dock and head southwest through the channel (marked on both the park brochure map and the NOAA chart) to Bird Key Bank. An actual key existed here before it was obliterated in a hurricane. Today this shallow sandy area provides excellent snorkeling and a good resting point before taking on the challenge of crossing the three miles of open water to Loggerhead Key. The route west-northwest across Southwest Channel is beautiful but can be overpowering if the tide is running. Paddling across on a calm day at slack tide is the way to go. Use your chart to leapfrog across shallow waters until you must take on the sixty-foot depths at midchannel. Then push and pull with your sights set firmly on the 150-foot spire of Loggerhead Key Light. A long white beach stretching the length of the key will welcome you, as will the sound of breaking waves pounding the reef. Relax and enjoy. Breathe in, smile out.

Check your watch and tide table. Calculate how much time you can spend before making the return trip. Add an hour just in case. Then, if you're lucky and you've got a spare hour, pull your boat up above the high-tide line and walk around to the northwest side of the island. Just offshore lies Little Africa. Put on your snorkel mask and flippers and head under the water. You'll find a magnificent spur-and-groove coral formation shaped like the continent it's named for. Look closely and you'll find a row of cannons completely encased in coral. That's something you don't see every day.

A walk around Loggerhead Key is also recommended. This island, so far removed from the mainland, is truly exceptional.

With enough time and good weather, you will find more superlatives in the waters of this remote national park. Keep safety in mind, both for yourself and the environment, and let wonder fill your days.

FYI:

Daily ferry service to Dry Tortugas National Park is available from

Sunny Days Catamarans
1326 10th Street
Key West, FL 33040
(305) 296-5556

and from

The Yankee Fleet
P.O. Box 5903-B
Key West, FL 33045
(305) 294-0939

Ten tent sites are available on a first-come-first-served basis (no water available; picnic tables, grills, saltwater toilets, and wheelbarrows for transporting goods available). Groups of ten or more must obtain permits in advance. Commercial tours are strictly regulated by advance permit.

Additional information on Dry Tortugas National Park is available from

Superintendent
Dry Tortugas National Park
P.O. Box 6208
Key West, FL 33041
www.nps.gov/drto

Dry Tortugas Ecological Reserve

A broad coalition of citizens, government agencies, environmental organizations, and commercial interest groups have worked to establish
the Tortugas Ecological Reserve. Based on a unanimous recommenda-
tion of the Advisory Council of the Florida Keys National Marine Sanctuary (in 1999), this reserve establishes a no-take fishing zone covering 191 square nautical miles. It includes national park waters and
such important areas as Sherwood's Forest, Riley's Hump, and one-
half of Tortugas Bank. Like past preservation efforts, the drive to establish this reserve was based on an abiding love of this fragile ecosystem, strong scientific support for limits on commercial and recreational
activities in such an environment, and relentless dedication by indi-
viduals committed to this corner of paradise. Unlike past preservation
efforts, this drive was broad-based, genial, and apparently unstop-
pable.

Tragically, three commercial vessels ran aground just off the western wall of Fort Jefferson in early 2002, releasing oil into these fragile
waters. Cleanup efforts began immediately.

Meanwhile, members of the Personal Watercraft Working Group of
the Florida Keys Marine Sanctuary are holding public forums on the
management of Jet Skis within all National Marine Sanctuary waters.
A new Florida state law, passed with heavy industry lobbying, prohib-
its localities from enforcing ordinances that single out personal watercraft. Reconciling this law with the sanctuary's mission of protecting
the Keys' natural resources is just the latest challenge faced by those
who venture on the water in this corner of paradise.

Index

Kathleen Patton has kayaked the backcountry and oceanic waters of the Florida Keys for many years. A certified diver and avid naturalist, Ms. Patton has published articles on kayaking, diving, and sailing in the Keys. Through her job as program coordinator for Florida Keys Discovery, a nonprofit community education project "exploring everything unique and wonderful about the Florida Keys," she continues learning and educating the public about the natural wonders of her island home. She lives near the patch reefs on Key West.

This is a very remote area. Check weather forecasts before committing to a kayak trip. If you plan on snorkeling, bring a partner, an anchor, a dive flag, and a length of strong rope. Be very careful to anchor in a sandy patch of seafloor. Never anchor on coral. Practice getting out of and back into your kayak in deep water before you take this trip. Don't venture from the shores of Garden Key if you are not confident of your paddling, swimming, or snorkeling ability or your ability to pull yourself into your kayak from deep water.

The Dry Tortugas are a group of seven coral and sand islands located seventy miles west of Key West. They were discovered in 1513 by Ponce de Leon and christened Las Tortugas for the prevalence of sea turtles. The adjective "dry" was quickly added to their name on nautical charts, letting sailors know that no fresh water could be found here.

Garden Key, the centerpiece of the hundred-square-mile Dry Tortugas National Park, is the site of a lighthouse built in 1825 to warn navigators away from the perilous offshore reefs. A second lighthouse was built on neighboring Loggerhead Key in 1856. In 1846 work began on Fort Jefferson, the "Gibraltar of the Gulf." Sixteen million bricks and thirty years of hard labor went into the construction of this hexagonal fortress, but it was never finished. During the Civil War it served as a prison for Union deserters and for Dr. Samuel Mudd, the physician who set the leg of Abraham Lincoln's assassin, John Wilkes Booth. Sporadic use by the U.S.

Decide for yourself, but for me this is as good as it gets. Once you're on the water, you'll see nothing but blue sky, white sand, and the thousand-shaded water of "America's Caribbean." There's precious little land here, just seven tiny coral isles—most of which are closed to humans. Underneath the sea are forests of staghorn coral, mounds of huge brain coral, and 442 species of fish. Birds, 280 species of them, fill the sea air. Three species of sea turtles are to be found here, as are rare white-tailed tropic birds, purple-mouthed morays, red-tailed triggerfish, and black coral. This is a very special place.

8. Lighthouse at Fort Jefferson

Navy and Marines followed, and for a brief time the islands were used as a quarantine station.

Although of marginal importance to humans, the islands have always been vitally important to bird and marine species. A hundred thousand sooty terns return annually to their nesting grounds in the Dry Tortugas—a migration that enticed John James Audubon to the area as early as